LOSING FRIENDS

M000009147

PUBLISHED BY THE SOCIAL AFFAIRS UNIT

LOSING FRIENDS

DIGBY ANDERSON

A Philosopher Between Personifications of Vice and Virtue
Sanmacchino Orazio

© The Social Affairs Unit
All rights reserved

British Library Cataloguing in Publication Data
A catalogue record of this book is available from the British Library

Social Affairs Unit publications represent the views of their individual authors,
not those of the Unit, its Trustees, Advisers or Director

Book production by Crowley Esmonde Limited
Printed and bound in the United Kingdom

Pictures:
Cover © Mike Caldwell/National Trust Photographic Library
Title page © Christie's Images/SuperStock
Page 12 © Rob Rayworth/Alamy
Page 32 © The Estate of Nancy Mitford
Page 56 © Paul Quagliana/Shooting Times
Page 72 © SuperStock
Page 98 © SuperStock
Page 120 © National Gallery of Scotland
Page 148 © The British Museum
Page 164 © David Hancock/Alamy
Page 174 © Digby Anderson
Page 196 © www.britainonview.com

ISBN 0 907631 94 0

Social Affairs Unit
314-322 Regent Street
London W1B 3BB
www.socialaffairsunit.org.uk

CONTENTS

ACKNOWLEDGEMENTS

The research for this book and its publication was made possible by a grant from the Lynde and Harry Bradley Foundation. My thanks to Hallmark for permission to reproduce their greeting card messages and for information about the card market; to Anne Atkins for help with the letters to an "agony aunt". These letters originally appeared in the *Daily Telegraph* and I have made every effort through her to ask for their authors' permission to use them. If we have been unable to contact any of them, I apologize.

Also thanks to all who talked with me about friendship, whether in formal interviews or not. Some of them were: John Monks, General Secretary of the Trades Union Congress; Professor Julius Gould, Chairman of the Social Affairs Unit; physicians, Dr Myles Harris, Dr James Le Fanu and Professor James McCormick; business and financial analysts, Professor Tim Congdon and Dr David Lascelles, Jamie Borwick (Chairman of Manganese Bronze Holdings plc) and Professor Elaine Sternberg; The Very Reverend John Simpson (at the time of interview) Dean of Canterbury Cathedral; John Greenwood, Chairman of John Williams and Co; Dr Robert Grant, University of Glasgow; Professor Tim Fuller, Colorado College; Professor Douglas Den Uyl of Liberty Fund Inc; Michael Mosbacher of the Social Affairs Unit; Dr David Green of Civitas, Peter Waterman, formerly of Hasbro; investment company director, Gary Shugg; Professor David Marsland, Brunel University; Professor Kenneth Minogue, London School of Economics; Professor Christie Davies of the University of Reading; Professor Anthony O'Hear of the University of Bradford; historian Dr Andrew Roberts; Revd Dr Peter Mullen, S. Michael's, Cornhill; Michael Ward; Dr David Womersley of Jesus College, Oxford and Judith Anderson. Dr Simon Green, Fellow of All Souls, Oxford, not only contributed in an interview but read various drafts and added extensive comments on them as did Revd Dr Charles King.

INTRODUCTION

Euripides, in *Orestes* declares:

> *"One loyal friend is worth 10,000 relatives"*.

If he is right, then it is of considerable importance if friendship is in danger; and I think, today it is. When I started research into friendship I thought the danger was that friendships today might be shallower than they used to be. I still think that is a danger. Judged from the way we talk and write about our friendships, they seem to be pathetic affairs compared to those of past ages. We have diluted friendship so that it is now largely a matter of recreation, passing an evening together plus sharing the odd minor confidence. We enjoy it but put little into it. By "put in" I do not mean to suggest that friendship is a sort of exercise demanding stressful activity. Indeed all the frantic effort in the world cannot manufacture a single genuine friendship. It is, though, or used to be, as with all things which we value, demanding of sacrifice.

However, during the research, I later found other dangers. Friendship, unlike the family and community is not accepted as an agreed foundation of society, as a legitimated publicly functioning institution. Even conservatively-inclined scholars who talk endlessly about "civil society" and the importance of social institutions between the individual and the state such as churches, neighbour-hoods and local communities rarely mention friendship. Left-inclined thinkers, who used to make so much of solidarity, fraternity and comradeship – which, admittedly are rather different from friendship – also ignore friendship. Indeed it begins to look as if there is something secret and even subversive about friendship today. When it comes into competition with the claims of the family or the state it gets short shrift. Fathers feel they ought to be at home in the evening carrying out their obligations to their wives and children, not in clubs or pubs carrying out their obligations to their friends.

Elderly people, about to retire, seek retirement homes in places where they might make friends, but think nothing about moving to those new homes and places a long way away from people who have been their friends for decades.

Modern ideologies such as egalitarianism or rights-based political correctness are the enemies of friendship because friendship is preferential; it chooses one person to advantage at the expense of another. Promoting a friend or giving one a tip-off about a company share is, today, considered wrong. Especially, friendship is hounded from work and politics where it is called favouritism and cronyism. Related to this is the gravest danger of all, which is that friendship is seldom seriously discussed. The Greeks, Romans and indeed one strong strand within Christianity thought friendship an essential part of the virtuous life and of public life and discussed it in an intelligent way. My aim in this book is to provoke a revival of that discussion. Obviously I believe in the particular ideas I argue in the book about friendship. But the fundamental reason they are argued is to reinstate friendship as a matter of public concern and conversation.

I should recognize here too, something which some may regard as grievous shortcoming. *Losing friends* is mostly about friendships between men. I don't regard it as grievous; it simply leaves open an opportunity for some lady to write about female friendships, and no doubt, a man would have been in trouble for daring to write about the other sex. But that is not the reason for omission. I am chiefly interested in comparing how friendships were discussed and valued in former times including antiquity and today. Nearly all the great writings in former times were about friendships between men. Had I written about contemporary female friendships, I would have nothing (much) to compare them with.

The ideas about friendship which I include come from three sources. First, from the literature about friendship. This is not vast but much of it is fascinating and not widely known. Some of it is inspirational. Second, I conducted interviews. These were mainly with people who had something to say about friendship and particular walks of life: doctors, soldiers, businessmen, academics, trades unionists, clergymen who talked about their experience of friendship in medicine, the armed services, business and finance, the university, employed work, and the church. Some of these interviews are explicitly mentioned as such; some gave ideas which entered the overall flow of the argument but are not directly quoted and ascribed. Third, I drew on my own experience of friendship. Although I regret the lack of public acknowledgment of friendship, it seems I am part of that tendency myself for I do not identify my own friends whose friendship is discussed in the book by name except those of them who are dead. The living friends know who they are and how important their friendship is.

None of these friends is responsible for the opinions put forward in the book, nor are the trustees and officers of the Social Affairs Unit.

Digby Anderson

The Greek philosopher Aristotle thought that friendship was the best thing in the world: "No-one would choose to live without friends even if he had all the other good things."[1] Yet it appears that some people today have no friends or no friends worthy of the name.

> *"It is not unusual to conduct a funeral where there is no-one present but me, the deceased and perhaps the deceased's solicitor. The deceased appears to have no family and no friends. It did not use to happen."*
> A priest from the Midlands

> *"Once people used to include in their wills up to two pages of carefully chosen gifts for legatees who were friends. It is rare now. And when friends are left legacies we will sometimes discover they have not written or made contact with their (deceased) friend for some ten years."*
> Senior administrator for a probate company

> *"I have told patients with cancer to think twice before they tell their friends about the nature of their disease, for my experience is that on learning of it many so-called friends will cease to visit the sick person."*
> A general practitioner from London

> My friends *"seem happy to forget about me when they don't need me...Could the situation be improved?"*

> *"I am thirty years old and I don't have a clue how to make friends."*
> From two letters to a daily newspaper agony aunt.

---

[1] Aristotle, *The ethics of Aristotle*, Book VIII, sect 1, Penguin, London, 1976, p 258

"Do you wish to travel on your own without being alone?...A Small World holiday is designed for you...Our House parties will welcome you as a friend rather than a paying guest – everyone is on first name terms from day one".

There are now several holiday companies which explicitly cater for single travellers who wish the company to organize the holiday so that it will be "sociable". They want the company to provide people, other travellers, strangers, in fact, who will, on arranged occasions act, as it were, as friends. There is also now an organization which provides volunteer visitors for hospitalized people who have no friends to visit them.

BBC radio has announced that British schools are introducing friendship classes because children no longer know how to make friends. *BBC Radio 4, 20 July 2001.*

CHAPTER ONE

THE PUZZLE OF FRIENDSHIP:
THE LOVE WHOSE NAME IS SELDOM SPOKEN

FRIENDS IN OBITUARIES

There are some people who have a genius for friendship. They are unusually good at both making and keeping friends. When they die, they may not be remembered for what they did with their careers at work or for any achievements in sports or civic duties. But they will be remembered for their genius at friendship. Or will they?

Their friends will of course remember both them and their capacity for friendship; but, possibly, no-one else will. Obituaries, for instance seldom mention friends and friendship. There are paragraphs on careers, substantial mentions of military service and school and university education. Inventions and innovations rate serious mention. For instance and as a more or less random example, *The Times*,[2] in its obituary of Edward Craven Walker, the inventor of the "lava lamp" also finds plenty of space to tell its readers and more generally to record for posterity:

---

[2] *The Times* (London), 21 August, 2000

> *"The other dominating interest in Walker's life was naturism, with which he had become acquainted in the South of France. He became a great advocate of the naturist philosophy and in 1960 shot the film* Travelling Light, *'an underwater ballet' featuring a naked swimming girl. It became the first of its kind to pass the censor for public viewing and was a considerable box-office success. Much of the money he originally made from it went towards the Bournemouth and District Naturist Centre, which he founded, and which set a standard for British naturist resorts."*

The Times does not find space to explain what this "standard" was. But, more to the point, it does not tell us anything about Mr Walker's friendships. Indeed, it does not even record whether he had any. It shows no interest in the matter at all. Perhaps it assumes its readers also have no interest. And perhaps it is correct.

In a similar way, the *Daily Telegraph*[3] records

> *"Mariga Guinness…promoted the Georgian cause and in Britain pioneered the renovation of early eighteenth-century Huguenot weavers' houses in Spitalfields in London's East End."*

If a deceased person is found ever to have said anything noble, apt or witty, it is faithfully recorded. Thus the same Mrs Guinness can rest assured that future generations will know she said,

> *"from the age of three, I have always been more impressed by buildings than people".*

She also spoke of "television machines". In contrast, the most we are told about friends is that the deceased had them and inspired or amused them.

---

[3] All *Telegraph* examples are from *The Daily Telegraph book of obituaries: a celebration of eccentric lives*, edited by Hugh Massingberd, Macmillan, London, 1995

If we take the obituaries of eccentric people as seeming to offer the most fruitful hunting ground, what do we find about the friendships of these people? Lord Huntley, it is explained, formed the House of Gordon Society to promote friendship among members. This short passage is positively verbose compared to the entry for the Very Reverend Hugh Heywood. He had "many friends". The Earl of Carnarvon had lots of pals. Julian Anthoine mountain-climbed with friends. It seems, though little detail is given, that he actually saved the lives of two friends. That is true friendship. Elsewhere in the obituaries the few mentions made of friends use that term in a way that includes acquaintances, companions and even regular customers. Arthur Lunn, who served in Fortnum and Mason for nearly sixty years, liked to think of his customers as "friends". He may have; they weren't. The book contains just one entry celebrating an actual friendship and its effect and that, interestingly, is in a postscript by the novelist Anthony Powell, to the entry for Adrian Daintrey. It briefly records their good times together, his "peculiar wit", his friendship with Augustus John and ends,

> "Daintrey ended his days in the Charterhouse where
> to the end he was visited by many charming young
> women. I have lost an old friend, and I do not doubt
> that Daintrey's passing will bring a tear to the eye
> of more than one lady of quality and black bus
> conductress."

Obituaries in the United States tend to conform to the same pattern as in England. Reasonably close observation of the obituaries in the only paper of a large Midwestern city show virtually no mention of friendship at all. The obituaries are written according to a sort of formula. People who have been politically, economically or socially prominent get a larger write-up, perhaps even with a photo. Nevertheless the extra information about them falls into the same categories. These include, in addition to the funeral arrangements, occupation with citation of positions held and titles, religious affiliation if any, schooling and degrees, clubs, societies and survivors. For survivors there is a strict formula as to who may be mentioned by name (spouse – and indeed serial spouses, children, step-children, parents, siblings and step-siblings) and who by number (grandchildren and great grandchildren). This information is gathered for the newspapers, except in the case of the wealthiest and most prominent people, by morticians. The staff at "funeral homes" have a form to be filled out. It contains all the above categories but has nothing for friends.[4]

When confronted with the censorship of friends and friendship, those who write the obituaries might well reply that friends are a personal or private matter and obituaries are about the public lives of public figures. But that is the point. In many previous societies friends were indeed public matters. Alasdair MacIntyre points out that, for Aristotle, the thing that binds the members of a *polis* or state together is friendship.

> *"Friendship is itself a virtue...[It] embodies a shared recognition of and a pursuit of the good...Friendship is more important than justice. Justice is the virtue of rewarding desert...within an already constituted community; friendship is required for that initial constitution."*[5]

Modern day morality is, in part, based on Aristotelian ethics. It follows him in thinking of courage, sincerity and justice as virtues. But with friendship the contrast could not be more stark. He makes it the foundation of society, of public-ness. We regard it as a private thing, indeed to be kept out of state affairs. He regards it as a virtue. We regard it as a recreation and comfort. He philosophizes about it. We very rarely talk systematically and explicitly about it. When

---

[4] PC Dr Charles King

[5] Alisdair MacIntyre, *After virtue*, Duckworth, London, 1981, pp 155-6

we do mention it, it is vaguely and ambiguously, blurring the boundaries between friends and companions, comrades, mates and flatterers.

The editor of the obituaries page of a large selling quality British newspaper had two explanations for this lack of explicit mention of friendship in the obituaries. He, as an editor, was not against substantial mention of friendship but the obituary writers did not seem to be able to write in an articulate way about friendships – beyond saying that the deceased had some. Further, if the deceased's long-term close friendship with someone or ones was emphasized, there was a danger the reader would think this meant he, or she, was homosexual. In the case of the American Midwest newspaper there was one case of a friend being mentioned among survivors. On being questioned, readers all assumed that this "friend" was a homosexual companion since he was of the same sex. Had he been of the opposite sex, they would have assumed she was a "live-in lover". Both writers and readers appear to have difficulty in understanding, accepting and articulating friendship.

Andrew Sullivan in a book on homosexuality and friendship, argues that friendship is the most common and natural relationship. We all have friends. That is highly disputable. But what he follows it with is not;

> *"And yet we hardly talk about [friendship]...*
> *The twentieth century has seen almost no theoretical*
> *exploration of friendship, no exposition of what it*
> *means, no defense of it, or even attack on it.*
> *Those modern writers who have ventured to deal with*
> *friendship have often done so in passing...One has to*
> *journey far...back, to ancient and mediaeval times, to*
> *glimpse a world where this relationship was given its*
> *full due and seen as something worth examining in its*

own right – as a critical social institution, as an
ennobling moral experience, as an immensely delicate
but essential interplay of the virtues required to sustain
a fully realized human being."[6]

Sullivan does not remark on the lack of mention of friendship in current obituaries. But he does remark that friendship, while often a quiet and reticent affair in practice, used to be very noisy when ended or threatened by death. Augustine's shout of grief at the death of his friend is echoed as noisily and eloquently by others such as Tennyson, Dr Johnson, Montaigne, Cicero and Aelred. There is something very new in not being able to talk about friendship even on the death of a dear friend.

FRIENDSHIPS NOT PUBLICLY RECOGNIZED: FRIENDS HAVE NO RIGHTS

Stay a while on the subject of death and friends. For friends do not fare much better, in terms of having a recorded place in society, immediately before they are obituarized. Picture a hospital bed, and a man in it dying. He has been involved in an accident and is in a coma. He is your friend and you are his. But the hospital does not contact you to say he has been admitted or tell you that he has only days maybe hours to live. Why should it? You are not next-of-kin, not family of any sort, *only* a friend. The hospital has no record of your friendship.

The man dies. And his surviving family, an older sister who saw nothing of him, a couple of cousins with whom he exchanged cards once a year at Christmas, and a nephew whom he loathed; they deal with the death certificate, instruct the undertakers, possibly talk to the priest and arrange the funeral. They may or may not invite the man's friends. They may not know who his friends are. They may know but decide to keep the funeral as "just family". You may,

---

6 Andrew Sullivan, *Love undetectable*, Vintage UK, 1999, pp 176-7

of course, go into the church during the service or walk up and stand behind the family at the graveside. No one can or will stop you. The service is public. Anyone may attend. But that is just it; you will be there as anyone. As a friend you have no automatic socially recognized right or responsibility to be there.

Some six months later, probate is granted, and the friend's estate is divided up and passed on. It is possible that he thoughtfully selected something for you, perhaps a book, a set of golf clubs, something to do with your friendship and mutual interests, to leave to you. But rarely are friends left substantial parts of the estate and often nothing at all. If they are left nothing they may never be told that that is the case or anything about the will at all.

At the funeral and perhaps on the anniversary of the death, the priest may pray for the dead man's soul and for his family and friends. He may well name the family. He is far less likely to name the friends. Why should he, any more than the hospital, know who the friends are?

It may not happen like this but it can and often does. And when it does there will be no public outrage at the exclusion – perhaps "omission" is a better word – of friends. This is not because, if asked to think about it, anyone would deny that, in this case and in many like it, the death is a bigger and more bitter blow to his good friend than to his semi-estranged and indifferent family. Saint Augustine describes what he felt when a friend of his died;

> *"grief...torment...misery...All that we had done together was now a grim ordeal without him. My eyes searched everywhere for him, but he was not there to be seen. I hated all the places we had known together, because he was not in them...I wondered that he should die and I remain alive, for I was his second self."*[7]

---

[7] Saint Augustine, *Confessions*, Penguin, London, 1981, IV 4 & 6

Friends can indeed be cruelly bereaved but their bereavement is a private matter.

The members of the family will be given time off work to attend the funeral. Close family may receive extended "compassionate leave". Other non-family will be expected to attend the funeral and get leave to do so; the dead person's head of department at work will be there. He scarcely knew him but he will represent the firm. But the friend, the dead man's "second-self" will have no automatic right to leave. And people will make allowances for the family, "she recently lost her brother, you know". But few will be made for the grieving friend. How would they know how to make allowances? Most would not know you were a grieving friend.

It is this lack of formal, public recognition which is the most extraordinary mark of friendship today. No-one doubts that friendship means a lot to friends and that the loss of a friend through death can be desolating. But friendship, its joys, sorrows, duties and rights are between friends – and their other friends. They are private matters. There are few rights or presumptions to friends' property or of access to the friends themselves in illness or imprisonment, though concessions may be negotiated. Friendships are not shored up in contracts and proclaimed by rituals open to society at large. MacIntyre notices how in some old heroic societies, friends take formal vows. Who my friend is, and indeed who my enemy is, is as clear for all in society to see as who my kinsman is. Often the vows effectively make the friend a kinsman with the rights and obligations that involves.[8]

Today, with the possible exception of schoolboy playground imitations of Red Indian blood brotherhood, there is not even a deliberate pact made by friends. In one sense, friendship is not then like the family, which is both a private and public institution. It is not a social institution.

---

[8] MacIntyre, *After virtue, op cit.* Ch 10

FRIENDSHIP AS SUBVERSIVE

It may even be an anti-social institution. Social institutions such as the family or the firm, the regiment or the team and indeed the nation state are wary of friendship. It is a potential rival to them. Men spend time at the pub when they should be at home with their wives and children. Soldiers may put their loyalty to their friends higher than their loyalty to the officer or regiment. The novelist E M Forster, in an essay published in 1938[9] famously imagined a situation in which he might have to choose between betraying his country and betraying his friends, and wished he would have the courage to betray his country.

Such an imagined conflict of loyalties is impossible in the Aristotelian world. If friends are united in virtue, who would want a traitor as a friend? But it is more complex than this. A proper country is founded not just on a piece of land with legal borders but on shared moral values, shared, according to Aristotle through friendship. One's country and one's friends are, in a sense, the same thing. They cannot compete for loyalty. If they do so, this can only be because "country" for men today has become little more than the place where I live and which protects me. The philosopher, Robert Grant, puts it like this,

> "If we assume that the said country is one worthy
> of allegiance, Forster's reasoning becomes almost
> unintelligible. For in the absence of a decent political
> order, such as the one to which Forster was subject,
> friendship is scarcely possible, since egoism is the only
> rational attitude to adopt. Friendship cannot trump its
> own indispensable condition. And the only case in
> which Forster's conflict could occur under a decent
> political order would be one in which the supposed
> friend was, in fact, a traitor. One who thus betrayed

---

[9] E M Forster, *Two cheers for democracy*, Edward Arnold, London, 1951

the very condition of friendship could hardly expect
to benefit from others' loyalty, or any longer to count
as a friend."[10]

There's another reason why Forster's conflict is odd. The historian Andrew Roberts in an interview for this book recalls the late John Aspinall saying that while he could not have a man as a friend who was a traitor, he could never betray a friend who was a murderer. The reason was that while he could imagine himself committing murder under certain circumstances, he himself could never be a traitor. This too recalls an ancient idea about friendship, that friends are other selves, people in whom we recognize ourselves.

Even today, although friendship may be seen as in rivalry with institutions such as the family or the state, it is also clear that it can help these social institutions. Loyalty to comrades can make and be used by those in command to make soldiers fight and endure suffering. Friendship has rescued many a marriage when passion has long departed. But friendship's help to these institutions is seldom acknowledged.

We are back again to the central fact that friendship is not publicly recorded. Of course many individuals might know Michael and Peter are friends but the friendship is not publicly available knowledge. And even those who know about it may not know what that friendship entails, how deep the ties are and in what they consist. Because it is largely unknown, it cannot be easily regulated – again something that authorities do not like. Individuals are free within certain limits to make friends as they wish and to make of those friendships what they wish. The price they pay for that freedom from society is to have no rights or privileges in society.

The anthropologist, Robert Brain sees one implication of this.[11] He points out that this is a comparatively unusual state of affairs.

---

10 Robert Grant, "Liberalism, value and social cohesion", in Zdenek Suda and Jiri Musil, *The meaning of liberalism: east and west*, Central European University Press, Budapest, 2000, note 6
11 Robert Brain, *Friends and lovers*, Paladin, 1977, Granada, pp 18-19

Many other non-modern but contemporary societies do make friendship a social institution with publicly enforced rights and obligations and rituals. He protests:

> "Why should we insist that love stand on its own two
> feet in the case of friends, when two romantic lovers
> who also love each other with all their heart, until
> death do them part, hedge in their passion with a
> wedding ceremony, oaths, and legal contracts.
> In denying friendship formal bonds our society seems
> to undervalue love, not value it. Even David and
> Jonathan made a pact. In mediaeval times friends made
> blood brotherhoods or, like Roland and Oliver, had
> a friendship of formal bonds based on courtesie."

The only survival of pacts would seem to be in childhood friendships. If today's children still read Mark Twain, it is possible some of them might imitate Tom Sawyer's and Huck Finn's pact:

> "[An initiation] is to swear to stand by one another, and
> never to tell the gang's secrets, even if you're chopped
> all to flinders, and kill anybody and all his family that
> hurts one of the gang...And all the swearing's got to be
> done at midnight, in the lonesomest, awfulest place you
> can find – a ha'nted house is best...and you've got to
> swear on a coffin, and sign it with blood." [12]

But it's more likely they would not be entirely serious and certainly Twain supposes we will be laughing at Tom and Huck.

PAST SOCIETIES WHICH GAVE SOME ACKNOWLEDGMENT TO FRIENDSHIP

One must also qualify Robert Brain's point and point out that societies such as that of the young American Republic or of

---

[12] Mark Twain, *The adventures of Tom Sawyer*, Airmont, 1962, p 221

Victorian England gave to friendship some public status even if it did not go as far as the public status accorded by Ciceronian Romans. Even that limited status has now declined. And the invisibility of friendship goes much further today. Robert Bellah has argued that the high notion of friendship associated with Cicero and Aristotle and seen by them as part of the public good was "well-known to Americans in colonial and early republican times".[13] The founders of the American republic, Washington and Madison, Adams and Jefferson were friends and committed to friendship as an ideal. Indeed two books on them are titled *Founding friendship* and *Founding brothers*.

In Victorian England nearly half the population of marriageable age was unmarried. Male friendships were an important part of life and provision was made for them in institutions such as gentlemen's clubs. I am not of course saying that all the members of such clubs were or are friends but that one role of the club is to provide a place where friends can meet and indeed where friendships *might* be made. Friendship was part of the public school education, the military ethos and the way much business was done. There were many genuine friendships among farmers and farm-labourers. The Friendly Societies had as one of their objectives, to provide an organized basis from which freely chosen friendships might grow among the workers who had moved to the new towns. And the considerable obligations of true friendship were widely if quietly understood.

FRIENDSHIP ONCE OF A SIMILAR IMPORTANCE TO MARRIAGE

When I say that friendship may be in especial danger in modern society, one response will be to say, "Surely, people today have lots of friends". One prominent and lofty socialist politician a few years ago had it suggested to him in an interview that he did not have any intimates. "Nonsense", he snorted, "I have thousands of friends".

---

13 Robert Bellah, "Reaching out", in *Habits of the heart*, Hutchinson, 1985, p 115

He may have done, indeed, but how many of them were of the sort Augustine was thinking of, other selves? How many friends do you have – true friends that is, not just people to chatter to – acquaintances – or seek amusement with, that is mates, but friends? One can get bogged down in the language; are companions and comrades friends? But for the time being I mean by friendship a serious relationship, the loss of which can cause the grief that Augustine speaks of; or, to look at it another way, a relationship of the same depth and quality as that of a good marriage. For it is precisely because friendship can be that serious and deep that it can become a rival to matrimonial loyalties. It's not just marriage that friendship can be ranked with or above. The American political philosopher Leo Strauss points out that Hiero, in Xenophon's *Hiero*, concludes that friendship has a higher value than city or fatherland or patriotism.[14] The point, at least for the moment is not which is more important, pleasurable or better. It is that for key past civilizations friendship was of the same sort of importance as the most important things in life and, as such, worth thought and explicit comment.

What are called "friendships" are plainly still popular. Not many people are eager to declare they have no friends. Being friendless reflects badly on one because there may be the inference that you are not the sort of person anyone wishes to be a friend of. But if we ask whether there are a significant number of people today without true friends, or whether our modern society is one in which friendship plays a diminishing role, I think the answers are yes.

The trouble with these questions is that because friendship, as we have seen, is not like marriage, a publicly acknowledged state, they are difficult to answer with the sort of evidence normally expected. However strong and long lasting John's friendship with Peter may be, however much self-sacrifice either puts into it, there is no public

---

[14] Leo Strauss, *On tyranny*, University of Chicago Press, Chicago, 1961

record. No register office legally establishes it. No church blesses it. There are no official witnesses to it. So no statistics exist of how many friendships succeed and fail today as compared to yesterday.

FRIENDSHIP DOES NOT HAVE THE QUALITIES IT ONCE HAD

There are, of course studies on friendship, or at least studies which claim to be of friendship. Thus for instance, a *British social attitudes; special international report*[15] asked whether friendship was as important to various nationalities as relatives. It took as one index how often a person met his friend or relative. And it found that people met friends more than relatives. But this tells us nothing about what they met for, about the quality of the relationship. One might reply that however often modern persons meet their "friends" they overwhelmingly put family first when it comes to matters such as leaving their estate on death.

Even if there were studies about friendship as distinct from companionship, they would help but little as the current controversy about the family shows. With the family there is an abundance of statistics showing the enormous increase in divorce and single parenthood. But those who support the traditional family and claim these as evidence of its decline are constantly told these figures show not decline but change. The one-parent divorced family and the homosexual family are merely new forms of family, we are told, and none the worse for it. There are apologists for all sorts of relationships including ones which would once have been thought perverted or the opposite of the family who now decree they are merely alternative family-like arrangements.

It is not so much a disagreement about the evidence as about definitions. And definitions are tied up with judgments and ideologies. Since "family" is taken to be a good thing, both traditionalists and those arguing for what would once have been

---

[15] *British social attitudes; special international report*, edited by Roger Jowell *et al*, Gower, 1989

viewed as perversions or anti-family arrangements are bidding for the right to use the word to describe their preferred choice. And so it would be with "friend". It too is widely regarded as a good thing. So even if friendships were statistically recorded, that would not produce agreement about the current state of friendship. You can imagine the debate. One side would show that today friendships are shorter lived than before; their opponents would reply that lots of short friendships are as valid a way of life as a smaller number of long-lasting ones. The first side would show that friendship in modern society was increasingly confined to leisure – a matter we shall return to – and unaccepted at work. "So what?" the opponents would reply. "Leisure is a very important aspect of modern life."

MODERN FRIENDSHIPS, MORE OF THEM BUT SHALLOWER

In fact, shortly after I had written these words, a book was published titled *On Friendship*.[16] Its author, sociologist Ray Pahl, accepts that "the great ages of friendship could be claimed to be in the past". But he prefers the view that "friendship is reaching new levels of depth and complexity in the modern world".[17] He does not claim that modern friendships reach those discussed or practised by Plato, Aristotle, Augustine, Aquinas, Aelred, Montaigne, Jeremy Taylor, Coleridge, Newman or C S Lewis. But he points out that these were confined to a small group of people by class and sex. Today, more people have friends. He may be right, but are these "friends" what writers of past ages would have considered friends? Are they what Aristotle would have called "a good"? Pahl suggests that past ideals of friendship cannot reasonably be expected to be fulfilled today because today's society is very different. This is a very sociological view. Aristotle might have replied that friendship is an excellence and no number of second bests can count for it. Moreover it is an excellence of man's nature and social change does not change that nature.

---

16 Ray Pahl, *On friendship*, Polity Press, Cambridge, 2000
17 *Ibid* p 69

Ray Pahl goes on to give an instance of what he evidently regards as a splendid modern friendship. Friends help us to "live in a way that in our hearts we find morally acceptable". They help us to "explore loyalty, trust and betrayal". This is already some way from traditional notions of friendship. These certainly value loyalty but scarcely value "exploring" it nor are many of them reliant on the impulse of "hearts". Pahl's example is Sue, a 35 year-old woman who has accumulated "friends" at school, college and job. Pahl makes much of the efforts she makes to maintain her friendships and this would fit with some traditional advice to keep friendship in repair. She has hour-long talks on the telephone, visits at weekends, drives hundreds of miles, writes letters, spends the night at friends' houses. She clearly talks to her "friends" a lot. They "pour out their inmost feelings to each other". Most friends stay but some come and go. One is about to be dumped because Sue has found he or she has racist views. But Sue's possible friendships are not limited by age, sex, race or sexual orientation. Pahl thinks it worth mentioning that one is a lesbian. The effort Sue puts into these friendships, she refers to as "managing" her friends. It is the same sort of vocabulary as "working at relationships". It is the language of heavy engineering rather than sacrifice and moral commitment. In return, the friends provide her with "continuity and support for her changing identity". Some of them are closer than others and one of the less close is "shaping up well" to become a close friend. The classical view would have been that friends should help us preserve our character and identity not change them.

Apart from the managing Sue does, there is far too much about what the friendships do for Sue, their functions, and too little about Sue's virtue in the friendship for this to fit classical friendship. Moreover a key aspect of classical friendship is permanence of character which sits ill with Sue's changing identity. This is important. For the reason why, in the classical conception, friends can trust each other is that friends are "other-selves" and friends have permanence of character. I can trust my friend as much as I can myself and I can trust him because he remains the same person with the same character that I made friends with. However enjoyable Sue's company may be and however much work she may put into managing her friendships, I cannot trust someone who does not remain the same person, someone who is changing her identity and on a continual exploration of emotions and morals. Also important, there is far too much about feelings and hearts and too much confusion of these with moral commitment.

It is certain that Sue is impeccably politically correct. She is also a sociable and friendly person. But I am not sure her life is strong evidence for the strength of friendship in modern society. But this sort of argument is not easily resolvable. And that is perhaps the most important point to note.

The test of cooking in France is not whether lots of cooking is done or even whether lots of people enjoy eating lots of meals there. It is whether France has a society which recognizes good – and bad – cooking. Whether Sue has lots of friends or not and whether there are many or few Sues in modern society is not nearly as important as the absence of agreement about what constitutes friendship. The fact that many of us, including it would seem Sue, cannot talk clearly, coherently and consensually about what friendship is, is much more evidence of a decline of friendship than Sue's success or failure at it. The true test is not *rates* of friendship but whether one could get substantial agreements of several friendships that some indeed were true, some not, some better, some worse. If it's "whatever suits you" then indeed it may be good for you but it is not a friendship in a social, a moral or a classical sense.

For the possibility must be that some or many of what are called friendships are no such thing. They may be other good things such as companionship or bad things such as mutual sources of flattery or cabals. Pahl does establish convincingly that friendship in a democratic modern society might be able to be wider than before. He asserts that it is also deeper and more complex. The depth he certainly does not establish. And perhaps "confused" might be a better description of modern friendship than "complex".

So it may not matter too much that we have little public evidence on the state of that informal, personal thing called friendship, or that the research on friendship, while useful on some quantitative matters such as asking teenagers how long their friendships last or how long it takes to make friends, fails to get to the heart of friendship, fails to show in any detail its qualitative change.

And qualitative change is the key. I contend that the friendships of today are simply thinner than before and increasingly restricted. By "thin" I mean there is less to them. By "restricted" I mean that friendships have been pushed out of key social institutions such as business and are increasingly seen as belonging to recreation. One sort of evidence is that friendship is increasingly viewed as a danger, for instance in teacher-pupil friendships or friendships in business. Another obvious sign is that friendship is no longer talked about or written about in a sophisticated way. Even institutions such as the family which are in serious trouble occupy acres of newsprint and social and political comment. That's true of community and even neighbourliness too. But not friendship.

The problem with "proving" the state modern friendship is in is not just a methodological one. It is certainly a nuisance not to be able to show in some clear and unambiguous way that friendship has declined or is alive and well. The problem is one that affects friendship itself. The fact that it is unrecorded, unrecognized, has few social institutions to support it and is not discussed in a sophisticated way is itself evidence of a *social* decline in friendship.

Take two further examples. Until the Second World War, gentlemen's clubs were institutions which sustained male friendships. Working Men's clubs did the same, for rather longer, for working class male friendships. Especially the gentlemen's clubs declined in the sixties and early seventies. They have now revived. But they are, arguably very different. It is not just that many of them admit members of both sexes. It is not even that they are now seen clearly to have little to do with deep male friendships. It is that their relationship with friendship is unknown and unrecognized. It is also, possibly, less legitimate. Gentlemen's clubs are much more popular at lunch times than in the evenings. The difference, of course, is that in the evening they have to compete with the demands of the family, demands increasingly thought to trump those of single sex friendship.

The second example is that of greetings cards. It needs a short chapter to itself.

Overleaf

Letter from Nancy Mitford to Evelyn Waugh asking for his advice on *Madame de Pompadour*

So many things I want to ask as I plod along.
References: a bibliography at the end? Not foot-
notes I think.
                    7. Rue Monsieur VII   19 Feb 53/.
                      Suffren 7665

Darling Evelyn
          You are faithful & clever. I'm sending
for all those books — & Ste Beuve's Port Royal
has been re published here.   I've always
known I must read that.   The enemy Brittannica
which I've got, is a help in a small way &
I do more or less grasp the functions of
the parlements but not how they are constituted
They seem to represent the King rather than
the people. Nobody here knows it IS SO ODD
Colonel hastens to change the subject — I
asked my lawyer who fled.

          Are you busy? If not, one word of
advice. Who am I writing for? Hamish
Ham wants me to do it as a novel & that I
won't (can't really) But I feel it's no good
doing it as though for, say, you & G M Young
because though you may read it in order to

CHAPTER TWO

TALKING TO FRIENDS ABOUT FRIENDSHIP:
THE CASE OF GREETINGS CARDS

The greeting card market is now bigger than the Cola market. The British send 50 cards per person per year and the Americans 25. And a huge section of it is occupied by cards which explicitly or implicitly are about friendship. This section itself is divided between more traditional cards and newer ones – new in the sense that they are not tied to occasions such as birthdays or new in that they have images associated with young people.

The cards described below were bought at an English card shop but similar ones are available in the USA. Indeed one American who studied cards both in the UK and US "found nothing English" about the ones on sale in England, not even the pictures of such things as thatched cottages and teddy bears. Indeed he remarked that the language on the English cards looked more like American than British English and suggested that if anything the cards were an American cultural tendency rather than a British one. The cards under discussion were produced by Hallmark. The company itself commented that a lot of the card images were generic but that some images were specifically English featuring, for instance a hedgehog – not known in the USA. Moreover the wording on generic international designed cards was specifically British. And American cards have more sentiment. So what is the culture of the cards?

Consider the following greeting card. It has a picture of a rose on it and is titled "Birthday Wishes For a Special Friend". Then come the lines:

> *Your friendship is special –*
> *in the way you share,*
> *in the support you give,*
> *in the thoughtfulness you show...*
>
> *On your birthday and always*
> *may happiness touch your life*
> *as warmly as you*
> *have touched the lives of others.*
>
> *With Best Wishes*
> *For a very*
> *Happy Birthday*

Classic Card Company
Copyright Hallmark Cards UK

Last there is an attribution:

> *"Special Thoughts" by Sandra Wall Armitage*

Or this one:

> *FOR A DEAR FRIEND*
>
> Picture of tea table in garden outside a thatched cottage acknowledged as Un Jour en Eté by Henri-Gaston Darien
>
> *Wishing you a day*
> *as special as you are,*

*as lovely as the thoughtful
things you do,
and as happy as the times
we share*

Happy Birthday   Copyright Hallmark Cards UK

Or this:

To a Special Friend
ON YOUR BIRTHDAY
Picture of two teddy bears sitting on a floral covered
armchair seen through a window of the card's first page

Same teddies on message page but faces only
*There is always one friend
who seems to listen
a little more closely,
care a little more sincerely,
give a little more lovingly...
Thank you for being*

*that kind of friend
to me.*

Happy Birthday!   Copyright Hallmark Cards UK

The messages on modern greetings cards follow quite closely some
of the traditional and even the classical themes associated with
friendship. So in these three one finds the emphasis on how special
friends are to each other that one can see also in Montaigne.
Friendship is not just what we do together it is to do with the
mutual attraction of personalities, who I am, who you are. Two of
the cards use the word "special", the third talks of "one friend who
seems to listen more closely...". The friends in the cards "share

happy times" as do at least the lower of Aristotle's friendships. They don't explicitly "love" each other but they "care" for each other.

And the cards emphasize, as do traditional treatments of friendship, the joys that friends have not only when together but when they *remember* those times together. Look at two more cards:

> *A BIRTHDAY MESSAGE*
> *For A Dear Friend*
> Picture of cheese, apple, beer on tray near discarded blazer and Panama on wooden bench by geraniums in pots near wheelbarrow outside cottage door acknowledged as "Lazy Days of Summer" Edgar Hodges
>
> Inside, etching of cottage
> *You're remembered today*
> *for so many things –*
> *Especially the warmth*
> *your friendship brings!*
>
> *Have A Very*   Classic Card Company
> *Happy Birthday*   Copyright Hallmark Cards UK

> *FOR MY*
> *SPECIAL FRIEND*
> *WITH LOVE*
> *ON YOUR BIRTHDAY*
> Picture of flowers
>
> *"Nothing is*
> *so sweetly*
> *remembered*
> *as time spent with*
> *a good friend."*

We share
so many memories together,
So many smiles,
that brighten up our days,
So many times
that keep us close forever,
Even when we go our separate...
And since we have
a friendship built on sharing,
Each happy time
we spend will always be

A warm reminder of
your special caring
And another cherished
memory for me.

Wishing You a
Wonderful Birthday   Copyright Hallmark Cards Inc

Some cards allude to the permanence of friendship:

Thinking
of You
ON YOUR
BIRTHDAY
"A birthday
is a special day,
a time
that's set apart
For thoughts of
special people
who are always
close in heart".

Flower

These wishes are sent
In a warm, loving way
To show
that you're thought of
Especially today...
And each special wish
Is for happiness, too
Today and tomorrow
And always, for you.

Happy Birthday...
Happiness Always

Copyright Hallmark Cards Inc

Another refers to the pleasure of giving as well as of receiving friendship:

For A
Dear Friend
Picture of two puppies, one has knocked over a pot of geraniums and has a geranium in his mouth, the other has his head on one side, he is sitting by three more pots of geraniums, acknowledged as "Mischief Makers!"
by E L Beckles

Inside another, different sort of dog, in front of a fireplace with a slipper in its mouth
Warm wishes are always a pleasure to send
To someone who's always been such a dear friend!

Have A Very Happy Birthday

Classic Card Company
Copyright Hallmark Cards UK

Yet another speaks of trust and loyalty through ups and downs, or rather of loyalty by one friend even when the other is having "bad days":

A BEST FRIEND
If someone were to ask me
what a best friend is,
there are lots of things I could say.
A best friend is the one
you can trust completely...
the one who listens to you,
laughs with you,
cares for you
on your good days
and your bad days.
A best friend
is one of the nicest things
that can happen to you...
because out of all the world,
you've been lucky enough
to find each other.
Picture of suns, moons, birds and butterflies

More birds and butterflies
I could go on and on
about what a best friend is,
but it's easiest
to simply say...
A best friend is you.
Tracy Donovan

More suns and birds
Between
You and Me   Copyright Hallmark Cards UK

The closest we come to the idea that friends bring out the (moral) best in each other is in the following:

> *Each time*
> *I think of you*
> *I think of someone*
> *who has influenced*
> *my life in so many*
> *positive ways.*
> *You've shown a lot*
> *of faith in me,*
> *and you've helped me*
> *find ways to work through*
> *some problems that*
> *otherwise might have*
> *made me give up*
>
> Same front page
> *Each time*
> *I think of you*
> *I remember your acceptance,*
> *your caring and your patience.*
> *I also remember*
> *how you've also shown*
> *your love.*
> Picture of hearts, suns and flowers
>
> Suns and stars
> *That's why each time*
> *I think of you,*
> *I think how happy*
> *and grateful I am*
> *to have you in my life.*
> Eva Allen

Between
You and Me   Copyright Hallmark Cards UK

This card also explicitly mentions "love". And the one that follows also explicitly mentions "serious" matters and difficulties in friendship:

You're Such
a Good friend
Today I want to
thank you.
Not for anything
really special
but just because…
Picture of flowers

Same flowers
…Just because you have
a great personality
that makes you
pleasant to be around.

Child's drawing of a car, road and house –
with flowers outside
…Just because
you are
so much fun…

Coffee cups and jug and two mugs
…but you know
when and how
to be serious.

Child's drawing of flowers in pots
Just because

I feel like
I can talk to you...

Picture of two telephones – not mobiles – off hook from
the mouthpieces of which emerge words
"hello
– did you see...
– it's so good to hear from you
– how have you been?
– what do you think?
How are you?
– do you want to meet
– lunch on Friday...
...about
pretty much
anything

Picture legs, book, sun hat on beach with starfish
You make
friendship seem like
no work at all...

Picture of notebooks, sunglasses, telephone, cup of tea
...and even though
that's the way
it should be,
not every friendship
is easy

Flowers, bird, sun
Although there are
so many
wonderful things about you,
I want to thank you

most of all
for just being you…

Table, two chairs, cup of tea, one portion of chocolate
cake on a plate with two – mauve – forks
…Because when you are
just being you
it's so naturally comfortable
being me.
Tara Centejo

Between
You and Me   Copyright Hallmark Cards UK

And another even seems about to do a full Aristotle and talk of a
shared moral outlook if in an unusual way:

For My friend

Picture of – I think – a sun
I like you.
We have the same
beliefs and values-
like a belief in chocolate,
SHOPPING, and cappuccino,
and the value of behaving OUTRAGEOUSLY!
I like you.
We have the same taste
in everything…almost!
You're my friend.
You make me LAUGH.
And I feel like acting crazy,
I know I can always
count on you!

When we get together,
we're a MAD, silly, wild
combination!
That's why I like you.
That's why
I'm glad you're my FRIEND.
R T Shaw

Between
You and Me
always   Copyright Hallmark Cards UK

And here are a few much shorter ones. I include them not because they have anything further to offer on friendship but because this sort of card is increasingly popular.

Cover two mice and a pair of spectacles

Inside
We always

seem
to see things
the same way

Out of the Blue   Copyright Hallmark Cards UK

Promise me you'll
never change
Childish drawing of smiling face

I love you
just as you are!

Out of the Blue   Copyright Hallmark Cards UK

Friends…
Picture of two persons – from rear – sitting on bench
by sea looking at a sailing boat

…that's us!

Out of the Blue   Copyright Hallmark Cards UK

Picture of wild cat – leopard? With mouth open from
which come the words "Moo!, Meow!, Baa!

Inside
*I'm just not myself
when you're not around!*

Out of the Blue   Copyright Hallmark Cards UK

Photo of a ginger cat sitting on a tortoise

Inside
*Friends come in all shapes and sizes…
…but you're the very best!*

Out of the Blue   Copyright Hallmark Cards UK

Picture of boy in bed by an enormous telephone

*JUST WANT TO SAY,
"THANKS FOR LISTENING"…*

*…AND LISTENING…
AND LISTENING…
AND LISTENING…
AND LISTENING…!*

Out of the Blue   Copyright Hallmark Cards UK

Picture in the style associated with children's drawings
of two people one holding umbrella over the other with
rain descending
I'm here if you need me.

Out of the Blue   Copyright Hallmark Cards UK

Picture of a person with his head stuck through a star
WHEN IT COMES TO FRIENDS...

......YOU'RE A STAR

Out of the Blue   Copyright Hallmark Cards UK

SIMILARITIES AND DIFFERENCES BETWEEN MODERN AND CLASSICAL FRIENDSHIPS

It might be as well to stress, what should be obvious, that the greetings cards are not, of course, written by friends to friends. They are written by the card manufacturers and their agents. In a sense they are works of fiction like novels, plays or poetry; they are lines written by one person for other people to "say", in this case send and "hear", that is receive. And as with good works of fiction they contain enough reality for the reader or sender to recognize them as true to life, and not just anyone's life but the lives of him or herself and the friend. They have to be true to the actual friendships people have. To make them true in this sense of realistic, the card companies do their market research and they know what sort of messages will appeal to card buyers, senders and receivers. In this respect they are unlike some novels, those in which the novelist gives us his view of the relationship between characters. The cards reflect, to the card manufacturers' best ability what they think the card buyers make of friendship.

The cards may seem rather feminine. One person remarked to me "how utterly feminine they are". They are bought by boys and men too; the owner of one card shop suggested a seventy-thirty proportion of female to male buyers. Hallmark themselves point out that 80 per cent are bought by women but that some of these are bought on behalf of other male and female members of the family and given, for instance, to a grandmother.

So what are these friendships like? If the cards mirror actual real-life friendships, what sort of features do the real-life friendships of the card senders and receivers have? Again, it might be simplistic but the first thing to note is that the senders and receivers do have a special category of relationship called friendship. They don't confuse it with business or family relationships or even acquaintanceships. And with their friends they talk to each other of trust, shared pleasure, confidentiality and several other characteristics of friendship.

Today's people may not be able to talk precisely about friendship but they can recognize it and several of the qualities they associate with it follow classical lines. There are also some differences with classical definitions of friendship. Except in the odd card there is nothing that could be called a shared moral outlook. There is plenty of shared outlook but little on moral outlook. It may well be that exchanging cards on an occasion such as a birthday is not the right time for putting the world to right, though even that is a modern view. Perhaps a more interesting divergence from the classical understanding of friendship is that the cards are mostly about good times. Some mention hard times but the friendship itself is a happy, enjoyable thing. And that is what most modern people would expect of friendship. Classical authors, by contrast are preoccupied with such matters as the sacrifices necessary for friendship or its cost. David and Jonathan's friendship exhibits a typically classical theme in the awful conflict of loyalties it presents.

MODERN FRIENDSHIP, AN ENJOYMENT

Presumably modern friends have conflicts of loyalties between, for instance, what they owe to parents and what they owe to friends. Sexual attraction can cause mayhem among groups of friends and jealousy and betrayal are not unknown. But there is little of this in the cards. Classical writers also dwelt on the obligations of their sort of friends to tell the unpleasant truth to each other. I asked social historian Simon Green about this and he was clear that the traditional or old-fashioned idea of friendship required a friend to be tough with his friend

> "It's one of the basic functions of friendship...a friend can and should be reprehending, ironic...a friend can be witty at your expense...Look at those letters between Larkin and Amis[18] sending each other up rotten..." (Green might have mentioned as well the letters between Nancy Mitford and Evelyn Waugh[19] to make the same point).

And this absence of harshness, this happiness, illustrated by smiling suns, is linked to another modern feature of the cards. They are largely about recreation, having a good time together *outside* work. There is little mention of work, politics, illness, public life or the economy. Again this seems thoroughly modern. The card makers have got it right; they know that modern friendship takes place largely in recreational time. This also contrasts with especially Roman concepts of friendship. It further means that modern friendship does not appear very well-anchored in the unpleasant realities of life. There is much talk of trust and helping each other but the actual tasks this might call for, the actual practices it might lead to at work or in public life, are difficult to get at. Modern friendship, in terms of practice, what people actually do, is centred on recreation. Hence the images in the cards of coffee mugs, chatting on the phone,

---

[18] *Selected letters of Philip Larkin 1940-85*, edited by Anthony Thwaite, Faber & Faber, London, 1982
[19] *The letters of Nancy Mitford and Evelyn Waugh*, edited by Charlotte Mosley, Hodder and Stoughton, London, 1996

toys, sailing boats, teddy bears, puppies with slippers, roses, thatched cottages, geraniums, suns, butterflies, sun hats, chocolate cake. The cards and their manufacturers have got this absolutely right. If modern friendship is centred on fun and affection then obviously that is what the cards should focus on if they are to be recognizable to today's people as being about the friendship they know and enjoy.

USING YOUR OWN OR SOMEONE ELSE'S WORDS

There is one last matter about cards and friendship. What are we to make of the modern friend using a card rather than writing a letter? What happens with a card is that a third party, the card-maker enters the relationship between the two friends. Does this turn what was a private matter into a public one? And at least some people display cards for yet other parties to see and read; whereas letters can be shown to others but they are more traditionally regarded as private. And does it make a difference to express your affection to a friend and call him a "special" friend, or unique friend not in your own words but in those of a third party whose same words are used by thousands of other friends?

Really traditional people might be shocked at expressing friendship at all, let alone in someone else's words. Simon Green again

> *"It's always wrong to be saying these things, if they're true you don't say them…To say them is to diminish them…If you were to say anything, and occasionally you would…by definition it would have to be in your own words…"*

To which one rejoinder might be, "Has not poetry often been used to express that which I feel better than I can say in my own words?" and another might be, "What if someone cannot say it at all in his or her own words? Is it not better that the friendship card provides a prompt and script? At least it enables the friendship to be celebrated rather than nothing being said at all." I have complained earlier in this book that modern friendship is not public enough. The cards can also be helpful here in providing a visible public convention about friendship. Simon Green follows Montaigne in arguing that friendship does not have to give its reasons but we have seen there are problems with societies which have no public language at all, no signs of friendship, no recognition of it. And while friends need not explain their friendship to each other, an argument can be made for much more public discussion of friendship.

If there were a more explicit, consensual moral understanding of friendship in modern society then it might be possible to have public statements of friendship which did not incur the scorn of traditionalists such as Simon Green. It is then, perhaps, not the public expression itself which is questionable but the expression in a cultural void.

Green certainly raises an important question about whether contemporary society distinguishes finely enough among the various degrees of confidential, personal, private, semi-public and public communications. It is important because if it is inept at this it may also be inept at distinguishing different relationships which include friendship. But I think the cards do a useful task in providing a public script for friendship. Overall they probably help the institution of friendship. What looking at the cards has done is reinforce two earlier conclusions about modern friendship. It is centred on recreation. And, if modern friends cannot express their friendship in their own words, then that surely shows us a society which is inarticulate about friendship.

A DIGRESSION: MALE AND FEMALE FRIENDSHIP

Discussing the cards, it was asked whether they were bought more by girls and women than by men. Presumably the question is important because at least some commentators think female friendships differ from male ones. Are they, for instance, more given to sentimentality? And if society is being increasingly feminized, might friendship be being sentimentalized? If the cards are, as claimed, "utterly feminine" yet bought by some boys and men then are men sending "utterly feminine" messages? Generally I have avoided discussion of whether male and female and indeed male-female friendships differ. There has been a view in the past that women were somehow not quite up to high friendship. The writer of the entry on friendship in the 1792 *Encyclopaedia Britannica* notes that some think

> *"women are incapable of sincerity or constancy in friendship"*

but himself thinks

> *"[Women] are in general possessed of a more exquisite sensibility, nicer delicacy of taste, and a juster sense of propriety, than we. Nor are they destitute of generosity, fidelity and firmness. But such qualities are peculiarly favourable to friendship...they render the heart susceptible of generous disinterested attachment."*[20]

This is similar to the idea that female friendships were different from male ones involving, for instance more confidence sharing and intimacy. Both ideas are further related to the view that women have different virtues to men. There is yet another development of this view that a man can start life by having "male" friendships with his male friends and end up having "female" friendships with them. A man might value conviviality more in younger years and mutual

---

[20] *Encyclopaedia Britannica*, J Moore, Dublin, 1790-1797, VII, 467-476

reflection and confidence in later years. In a paper on Coleridge and friendship – which contains some of the above points and references – Gurion Taussig[21] suggests Coleridge understood friendship both in male-fidelity and female-exquisite-sensibility terms at different times in his life.

I suppose one might ask whether the exquisite sensibility mode of friendship is more susceptible to sentimentality than the fidelity mode, at least in the case of someone without Coleridge's analytic and reflective ability. But I shall not pursue it or the more general matter of male and female friendship. This is partly because it, like any other subdivision of friendship merits a book on its own. But it is also because my purpose is to revive an interest in friendship. The pursuit of different friendships, male and female, young and old, urban and rural, bourgeois and working class, French and English can so easily become a rhetorical device for suggesting there is no such thing as friendship, that is no *one* thing, there can be no decline or advance in it and there is consequently nothing to revive. What purports to be a sophistication and elaboration of our under-standing of friendship can so easily – and with malice afore-thought – become its anarchic destruction. Indeed that is how social science assisted in the destruction of the family.

YOUNG PEOPLE AND FRIENDSHIP

Many of the greetings cards are exchanged between young people and several features of the cards can be compared with academic research findings on contemporary friendships of young people. Michael Day surveyed the literature up to the late 1980s and conducted his own research on friendship.[22] He establishes first the popularity of friendship:

> *"We can be left in no doubt of the universal importance of friendship to young people…94 per cent of all young*

---

21 Gurion Taussig, "Idea and substance; Coleridge, Thomas Poole and the gendering of male friendship", *The Coleridge Bulletin* New Series 15, Spring 2000, pp 41-55
22 Michael Day, *Adolescence; the importance of the peer group and friendship*, PhD thesis, Brunel University, 1987

*people regard having friends as very important or
important…only one per cent thought it unimportant.
[Asked what they considered they liked about their best
friends, the young people gave a clear idea about the
quality of their friendships.] The first four items in the
rank ordering were:*

*1. Laugh, good laugh, joke, playing about, amusing,
cheerful; 25.8 per cent.
2. Trust, trusting/worthy, honest, loyal, sensible,
serious, reliable, tells truth, mature, acts intelligently;
15.3 per cent.
3. Helps you, helps with problems, kind, sticks up for
you, generous; 15.0 per cent.
4. Good company, good friend/mate, friendly, enjoy
each other's company, like to go around with, easy
to get on with: 9.4 per cent."*

The trouble is that Michael Day does not probe how deep these
qualities go: "The research does not indicate how far the bond can
be strained before a break occurs." To know this is, curiously,
important for enemies and occasional companions as well as friends.
Was it David Niven who said of Errol Flynn,

*"You know where you are with Errol; he always lets
you down"?*[23]

Permanence of character is important way beyond the confines of
friendship. Day does find what looks like a more moral expectation
of friendship in the emphasis on honesty and trust. He also finds
that friendship originates not only in leisure but in school. If school
is thought the young people's equivalent of work then this could be
important for the consideration of whether modern friendship is
exclusively a recreational affair. What one would need to know to

---

[23] *Personal communication* Simon Green

make it important would be whether friendships simply occurred at school or whether they were an acknowledged, legitimate way of doing work at school. The interesting question is not whether friendships can happen at work, school, in armies or hospitals. Of course they can. It is whether they are acknowledged and become public as well as private affairs or even conventional rather than subversive affairs. The very fact that Michael Day had to work so hard to find out about friendships testifies to their unpublic, uninstitutionalised character.

Even the mention of moral qualities does not establish that the friendships are indeed based in shared virtue. It is noteworthy that trust and honesty are what the young people say they give to as well as receive from friendship. But then they would, wouldn't they? We have already seen that if modern friendships are indeed less profound than classical high friendships, that need not prevent them following the *form* and language of high friendships.

Michael Day is right. Friendship is very popular. It is valued. When asked what they value in it, people will indeed use some of the words associated with classical and high friendships, words such as trust and loyalty. But that also might be the case if modern friendships were shallow and restricted in scope. The case of the family shows how the decline of the institution itself can be accompanied by a rise in the sentimentalised rhetoric associated with it. Never has a society gushed more about love and family relationships. That says nothing about the actual practice of love and the number of wives and children casually deserted.

What the cards and Day's research do show, without any doubt is the elusiveness of friendship or the "puzzle of friendship". And that will be a persistent theme of this book. Given the absence of "hard" evidence about qualitative decline in friendship, the most obvious place to start an analysis is with one's own experience or with the experience of one's friends. That too might be the way to understand something of what distinguishes true friendship from the relationship of two "friends" who simply play squash or drink together on Thursdays. We don't have to go back many years to get an idea of what true friendship was like.

CHAPTER THREE

FRIENDSHIP AS IT WAS:
BRINGING OUT THE BEST IN EACH OTHER

A FRIENDSHIP 1930-1980

Towards the end of the 1980s Eddie Ward died. He and his wife
Mary were old friends of my mother and father. Eddie outlived most
of his family and friends and that included my own parents. Which
is why, perhaps, his son asked me to say a few words at his funeral.
To my knowledge Eddie had had no specific religious beliefs. He had
certainly been a good husband and father but that was not something for me to say. It is revealing that the thing that ought to be
said took some time to strike me and even then was first dismissed
as trivial. Eddie had been a good friend.

He had been friends with my parents for some forty years. He and
my father had shot duck and pheasant together, golfed together,
drunk in the pub together. With the two wives, they had gone on
holiday together, shared dinner and cards and roulette at Christmas,
birthdays and anniversaries. My mother had met Mary almost daily
for coffee or tea. Perhaps more than the men, they had exchanged

worries and confidences about their children, money or illness. Mary had sat through the night with my mother during her dying days.

The two men shared more than pastimes. What started as companionship became something very different. They shared and reinforced a certain morality. There was not much difference between what each of them might have meant in describing someone else as a "decent" man or the reverse. When one thought so and so was a shocking old bugger, the other would have agreed and for the same reasons too. While each might have led the other on to have another drink or another bet on a horse, at a more serious level each reinforced what was best in the other. In Aristotle's classic analysis of friendship, he identifies three sorts and levels. There is friendship in which the friends seek pleasure, friendship in which they seek advantage or utility in business, and friendship which is grounded in shared morality or virtue. The last is true friendship. And Eddie and my father's friendship, though neither of them would have known much about Aristotle, had something else the Greeks associated with friendship. Had one of them done something the other disapproved of, the other would have told him. They were good enough friends to be honest with each other. The Greek understanding of friendship knew that flatterers were not the same as friends, indeed the contrary. Eddie and my father were not toadies but true friends. They spoke openly to each other. Both the Greeks and the Romans associated frankness of speech with friendship. Seneca writes

> *"Speak as boldly with [your friend] as with yourself...*
> *Share with [him] at least all your worries and*
> *reflections...Why need I keep back any words in*
> *the presence of a friend?"*[24]

This understanding was not entirely lost to the moderns. Earlier it was mentioned that the young American republic knew about classical friendship and its chronicler de Tocqueville, right at the

---

[24] Seneca *Ad Lucilium epistulae morales*, Richard M Gummere, Wilham Heinemann, New York, 1925, Vol 1, p 11

beginning of *Democracy in America* makes the point that only friends can tell the truth.[25]

HONESTY, SINCERITY AND PERMANENCE OF CHARACTER

In the Greek understanding, friendship was not just a staple of the virtuous life. Friendship could only work with the help of the virtues. These centrally included honesty and sincerity, but also trust, loyalty and what is well called "permanence of character". Slowly we start to see just how embedded in morality the idea of true friendship is and how different from purely utilitarian or recreational companionship it is. Sincerity, trust, loyalty and "permanence of character" Eddie and Father had too.

Further, I think, though it must be no more than a guess, that if out fishing or shooting, one had had some sort of accident, fallen over board or whatever, the other would have risked his life for his friend. Had some third party sought confidences from one of the friends about the other, confidences which might have enriched or advantaged the first friend, he would have been curtly refused. On the other hand, had either friend the opportunity practically to help the other in business or some other matter, he would have done so, always provided it did not breach a morality which, anyway, as friends, they shared. The great Roman writer on friendship, Cicero,[26] sees such help or "advantage" as a natural and welcome outcome of friendship. It was of benefit not only to the friends but to public life as well. One should not make friends with someone in order to secure an advantage. But once friendship is established it is right and natural that each should receive and give advantage and practical help. This matter of advantage and morality is vital. Cicero is not an apologist for the mafia. The behaviour of friends never breaches common morality unlike the favours of the international brotherhood or the particular affections of societies such as the Apostles (considered in chapter 9).

---

25 Alexis de Tocqueville, *Democracy in America*, Vol 2, 1845
26 Cicero, "Laelius: on friendship", *On the good life*, 6.20, Penguin, London, 1971

Cicero also saw a main function of friends as giving advice to the other and that too would have been characteristic of Eddie and Father's friendship.

There is certainly room to argue about the degree to which their friendship satisfies all these classical requirements. But it clearly exhibits to some degree the characteristics of shared moral commitment, self-sacrifice, trust, sincerity, loyalty, advice, confidentiality, advantage, a resort in time of need, and pleasure taken together as well.

Only in one aspect can I see that the friendship is much less than classical strictures would demand. These two friends did not talk much together of their fundamental feelings let alone talk about the friendship itself. But then they were Englishmen not Athenians, and middle-class provincial, south-eastern Englishmen to boot. I don't think they talked much about such matters to their wives either and that did not diminish their marriages. And there is a thought. So much of what friendship was to them could also be said to characterize their marriages. Both men would be horrified at the mention of the word but it is very difficult to avoid it; they *loved* each other. In this age when homosexuality is tolerated and even "affirmed", but when friendship is neglected, undiscussed and misunderstood, it is surely the relationship of people like Eddie and my father that can claim the title, "the love that dare not speak its name". Indeed now that the old, once unmentionable "F-word" falls daily from so many lips, friendship can claim to be the new, unmentionable "F-word".

ONCE FRIENDS SHARED A LARGE NUMBER OF FRIENDS

It involved more than each other. During most of the forty years of friendship, my father lived in one of the main streets of a small seaside town in Kent. Eddie lived, at least for some time, at the other end of the same street. My parents were friends, perhaps not quite so good friends but good friends with at least six other couples in the same street and three or four elsewhere. Eddie and Mary were also friends of more than half of these. Some modern commentators might be keen to see this as an example of small town community. It was certainly a small town. But this was no "community" in the sense they would like it to mean. Father and mother were friends with the six couples and that means there were some fifty or more other couples they were not friends with. They were not friends with anyone just because they lived close to them or did business together. There were even people, Father might have drunk, fished or shot with who were in no way friends in the way he was friends with Eddie and the other six. Call them acquaintances. My parents also had family, most of it quite a way distant, but their daily life, its purpose and affections were rooted not in wider family or community but in friendship.

Such friendships are not often passed on between the generations. I was not friends with the children of the six families except in two cases. This was not because many of us were at different boarding schools or because the families moved away. It was because the children of the families differed in age up to some five or more years and age matters much more for juvenile than adult friendships. But two of the children were and still are friends despite extensive physical distance.

What was interesting about the adults' friendships was that they were essentially friendships of couples. The husbands golfed or Rotaried together, the wives played bridge and went to church to-gether and the couples went to the races or on holiday together. And all this combined friendship involving, with the overlaps and children, twenty to thirty people at varying different times went on for some forty years during which half of them remained fairly constant.

The other personal source of knowledge about friendship comes from my own friends. Two date from the six families. One is from school formed at the age of eight. Another the daughter of family friends not from the seaside town. Another from past jobs. Three or four more from people my wife and I have met. Yet two or three more are friends made at particular times and places and held on ice. There is much controversy in the friendship literature about the effects of physical separation on friendship. My own experience is that true friendships are not threatened. They go on ice and when the friends are reunited the friendship continues as though it had never been interrupted. It may even be enhanced.

What is noticeable about my, and I think my generation's friendships as distinct from those of the previous generation, is that few are friendships of couples. And that has nothing to do with the personalities involved still less community or lack of it. It has everything to do with divorce. Not one of the couples who were my parents' friends was involved in divorce or separation. Another notable difference is that generally, weddings, funerals and parties apart, my generation does not mix its friends. It takes them one at a time or occasion. My parents' friends, as I have explained were part of an overlapping large set.

DAVID AND JONATHAN

I have deliberately started with an instance of a friendship which is comparatively recent and actually achieved – not some mere ideal. Let us now consider some other older instances. The first at least purports to be factual and it is the story of the friendship between Jonathan, the son of Saul, the king of Israel, and David. It begins after David has killed Goliath, champion of Israel's enemies, the Philistines. Initially grateful to David, Saul becomes jealous of David's fame as a warrior. David goes into hiding and Saul pursues him, to kill him. He looks for help from his son, but Jonathan has become David's friend and helps him rather than his father.

The actual friendship is described in five or six short verses only. Its beginning takes up less than twenty words. On returning to Jerusalem after the contest with Goliath, David met King Saul and his son Jonathan and there, we learn, David and Jonathan became friends;

> *"the soul of Jonathan was knit (the Hebrew is about 'binding') with the soul of David and Jonathan loved David as his own soul".*[27]

What sort of friendship was this? It may seem obvious but we should note that David and Jonathan are said to "love" each other. Whatever this means, it puts friendship in the league with other things people love such as their country, their husband or wife and their children. And indeed themselves. David and Jonathan find as much satisfaction giving pleasure to the other as to themselves and they become one soul. The language is curiously close to the Church of England Prayer Book Solemnization of Matrimony which talks of husband and wife being "knit" together. We are again told (ch20, v17) that Jonathan "loved [David] as he loved his own soul" and that he "delighted much in David" (ch19, v2).

The friendship was not a homosexual one and obviously was not, as marriage was said to be, for the procreation of children. But it did have a physical side. They found, again in the words of the marriage service, "help" and "comfort" in each other's company. That love and delight was expressed physically,

> *"they kissed one another and wept one with another".*
> (ch20, v41)

As with marriage, Jonathan was totally committed to David,

> *"Whatsoever thy soul desireth I will even do it for thee".*
> (ch 20, v4)

---

[27] I Samuel: ch18, v1 Authorized Version of *The Bible*

They pledged their friendship in the name of God and it was to be, as with marriage, indissoluble;

"we have sworn both of us in the name of the Lord...
for ever". (ch20, v42)

Their actions, especially Jonathan's, tell us a little more than their words. Jonathan stood by David to the point of risking his inheritance and his life. His friendship conflicted with his obligation to his family, in the person of his father, and to his country in the person of the king. Without going into detail, it is clear that the obligations of friendship did not come before those to family and country simply because they were obligations of friendship but because the actions of Saul, the father and king, were wrong in the sight of God.

GREEK AND ROMAN FRIENDSHIP CONTRASTED WITH MODERN FRIENDSHIP

If this sort of friendship is taken as a model, like the Aristotelian and Ciceronian models of friendship it gives some fairly daunting answers to the questions that might be asked about friendship today. Is friendship mostly a matter of spending leisure time enjoying ourselves together? No, it is about a commitment even to death and for ever. It costs the friends dearly. Nor does friendship end with taking leisure together; its obligations can run through work or politics. Are friends people who get along well together? Yes they do have "affinity" but it is more than that; they love each other. They feel each other's joy and grief as if it were their own. What happens when loyalty to friends clashes with loyalty to my family or country? That depends which cause is good or virtuous. Which is why E M Forster was not so much unpatriotic as morally ignorant.

This sort of friendship is not some pleasant undemanding pleasure, but a bond in the same sort of class as that of marriage, parenthood, religion or political conviction. And it is not confined to the Old Testament. C S Lewis has argued that the Greek and Roman friendships already discussed were, for them, the "happiest and most fully human of loves."[28] They bound men together and the highest form of such friendships was not based on mutual advantage or pleasure taken together, but on virtue. Jeremy Taylor the seventeenth century divine, in his tract on Christian friendship, explains that the reason we find little explicitly on friendship in the New Testament is that friendship is simply charity or love and the more we love our friends, and the more friends we have, the better we shall be, and the closer to God.

What we might call the classical understanding of friendship rates friendship very highly. But one does not have to take on all the classical understandings of friendship, the particular understandings of virtue for example, in order to rate it highly. Here is Coleridge writing of his friendship with Southey:

> "On what grounds...did I form friendship with him? Because our pursuits were similar, our final aspirations similar, and because I saw plainly, that compared with the mass of men Southey was pure in his Habits habitually indignant at oppression...Not that he was perfection; but because he was a far better man, than the vast majority of young men, whom I knew."[29]

For Montaigne friendship is based on the personalities of the friends

> "If I were pressed to say why I love [him], I feel that my only reply could be: Because it was he, because it was I."[30]

Bacon says that the listening friend soothes and opens the heart, aids the understanding and judgment and can act for his friend.[31] Bacon and Montaigne are very different to Aristotle in their understanding of friendship but not far at all in their rating of it. In that they are at

---

28 C S Lewis, *The four loves*, Fontana, London, 1960, p 55
29 Discussed in Reggie Watters, "Coleridge, female friendship" and "Lines written at Shurton bars", *The Coleridge Bulletin, op cit* pp 7-8
30 Michel de Montaigne, *Essays*, trans J M Cohen, Harmondsworth, Penguin, 1997, p 97
31 Francis Bacon, *Essays*, Dent, London, 1968, p 81

odds with today's society and not only in that. For they recognize friendship and describe it in detail and coherently.

DR JOHNSON AND CARDINAL NEWMAN

And there are two more people to look at to see just how far removed are today's thinking and practice of friendship from what once happened. These two both wrote about and practised friendship. They are Samuel Johnson and John Henry Newman. Johnson's friendship is, at first sight, a welcome corrective to the very high-minded conceptions of it associated with Aristotle or that exemplified by Jonathan and David. With Johnson one immediately thinks of conviviality. Johnson eats with his friends, sometimes fourteen dishes, soups, joints of mutton and beef, puddings. When he was drinking, he drank with them, once at Oxford, thirty six glasses of port. He joked with them as they ate and drank, often about eating and drinking. Once famously into his third bottle, he was unable to pronounce a word he wanted to say. After three attempts he finally succeeded. Then wisely said, "Well, I think it is now time to go to bed." When he stopped drinking alcohol, he drank tea excessively. He talked with his friends, expansively, competitively in vast jousts of argument and teasing. One night after a battling conversation at the Crown and Anchor, Johnson said to Boswell, "Well, we had good talk", and Boswell replied, "Yes, sir, you tossed and gored several persons".

He was a giant of comedy. Fanny Burney found in him

"more fun and comical humour, and love of nonsense...than almost anybody I ever saw".

Garrick said of him to Boswell

"Rabelais and all other wits, are nothing compared to him;...Johnson gives you a forcible hug and shakes laughter out of you whether you will or no".

Significantly his companions laughed with him in affection. Robert Lynd who lists these and other testimonies to Johnson also writes,

> *"We laugh with him...because he engages our*
> *sympathies...he is the perfect boon companion...In him*
> *goodness became convivial and grandeur of soul took*
> *its ease in the tavern. In his conversation, virtue holds a*
> *carnival, and wisdom is at once sociable and riotous".*[32]

For Johnson could take virtue seriously. Hume's infidelity shocked him; "those who write against religion ought not to be treated with gentleness". He could combine wit and piety; Sunday "should be different from another day. People may walk, but not throw stones at birds". He loved Boswell as a convivial companion but also "as a man of exemplary piety".

Johnson had lots of friends, some like Edmund Hector and John Taylor dating from his youth. He followed his own advice to Joshua Reynolds that friendships need to be kept in constant repair. Johnson also followed the classic advice and was frank with his friends to the point of rudeness. He knew the difference, as did the ancients, between friendship and flattery. Of Samuel Richardson, he remarked that he "could not be contented to sail down the stream of reputation, without longing to taste the froth from every stroke of the oar". Richardson died of the monotony of listening to the same flatterers "like a man obliged to breathe the same air till it is exhausted". It is important to note that he was not with his friends all the time. The Johnson-Boswell friendship lasted just over twenty years yet it is estimated the periods they were living near each other amounted only to two years and on most days in those years they did not see each other. Friendship does not mean constantly meeting but the friendship must be constant and Johnson's were. Even more important he remained constant in character. Lynd writes on Taylor and Johnson:

---

[32] Robert Lynd, *Dr Johnson and company*, Penguin, Harmondsworth, 1946

*"There could be no finer symbol of the unchangeableness
of Dr Johnson himself…than the fact that it was his
friend of boyhood, whom he summoned, when they
were both old men to pray at his deathbed…Johnson…
never forgot an old friend."*

It would be silly to claim that Aristotle's virtues and Johnson's were
identical or their views of friendship. However although Johnson
may at first seem very different and perhaps more attractive and
amusing, there is substantial overlap in piety and virtue, on giving in
friendship, on sympathy, constancy, frankness. And even on
marriage. Johnson seems to have placed friendship at least as high as
marriage and had decidedly unromantic views on the latter;

*"I believe marriages would in general be as happy and
often more so, if they were all made by the Lord
Chancellor upon a due consideration of characters and
circumstances without the parties having any choice in
the matter".*

There is no doubt that Johnson had a high, demanding and coherent
view about friendship and that places him with Aristotle and others
and over and against the thoughts and practices of the present age.

Newman's views on friendship we shall encounter later. But his
practice of it cannot go unnoticed in a chapter seeking to establish
contrasts with today for it is about as high as you can get. He made
and kept many friends in both his Anglican and Roman Catholic
days. The number is remarkable but not so remarkable as the depth
of the friendships. He closes *Apologia pro vita sua* in 1864 with the
following testimony to his friends,

*"I close this history…as a memorial of affection and
gratitude…to my dearest brothers of this House, the
Priests of the Birmingham Oratory, Ambrose St John,*

*Henry Austen Mills, Henry Bittleston… who have been
so faithful to me; who have been so sensitive to my
needs; who have been so indulgent to my failings; who
have carried me through so many trials; who have
grudged no sacrifice, if I asked for it; who have been
so cheerful under discouragements of my causing;
who have done so many good works and let me have
the credit for them; – with whom I have lived so long,
with whom I hope to die.*

*And especially to you, dear Ambrose St John; whom
God gave me, when He took away everyone else; who
are the link between my old life and my new; who have
now for twenty one years been so devoted to me, so
patient, so zealous, so tender; who have let me lean so
hard upon you; who have watched me so narrowly;
who have never thought of yourself, if I was in
question.*

*And in you I gather up and bear in memory those
familiar affectionate companions and counsellors, who
in Oxford were given to me, one after the other, to be
my daily solace and relief; and of all those others, of
great name and high example, who were my thorough
friends, and showed me true attachment in times long
past…And I earnestly pray for this whole company,
with a hope against hope, that all of us, who once were
so united, and so happy in our union, may even now be
brought at length, by the Power of the Divine Will,
into One Fold and under One Shepherd.* "[33]

Honesty, sincerity, constancy of character, loyalty, a shared morality,
a relationship sought for itself and not for advantage – though it
may result in it, a source of advice, self-sacrifice but also the love of

---

[33] J H Newman, *Apologia pro vita sua*, final page, Collins Fontana, London, 1969

self in another, pleasure, pastimes shared, conviviality, conversation, humour, infectious spirits, affinity, patience, tenderness; that's the high view of friendship. And somehow, in this view, what would now be called the "fun" side of friendship and any other advantages are tied up with the shared moral life. For Aristotle and the others, friendship was a virtue or a love, sometimes both.

"Friendship" as commonly used today is a word that has been somewhat devalued. But it is not the only word to suffer such a fate. Other words linked to it have also been degraded. Say "intercourse" or "relations" to the coarse modern ear and it is only too prepared to hear "sexual intercourse" and "sexual relations". "Love" has suffered a more complicated fate. It too can be heard coarsely as physical sex but it has also been sentimentalized into a sickly mutual niceness. Perhaps, because of this, some of those who write today on friendship never mention love at all. How strange to find sociological and psychological texts on friendship running to hundreds of pages with no mention of love at all. How sad to see the modern pseudo-scientific reduction of love to "relationships" which can be studied, advised on and therapized.

CHAPTER FOUR

THE DECLINE OF FRIENDSHIP: LETTERS TO AN AGONY AUNT

FRIENDSHIP STILL VALUED BUT IGNORANCE ABOUT ITS NATURE AND DEMANDS

How do contemporary friendships, those of the generations born in the second half of the twentieth century, compare with those described by Aristotle, Cicero, the Bible, Coleridge, Bacon and Lamb or those much later such as experienced by my father and Eddie? Again I will introduce some personal accounts. In a letter to what Americans call "advice columnists" and what the English call "agony aunts" a deeply worried person writes,[34]

> *"I have three friends I value very much. However, they seem unaware of the implications of good friendship. They are often highly critical of me, in addition, they frequently let me down badly with no qualms. Recently, I waited in almost all day for them to call, before discovering that they had arranged something better with someone else. I love being with them very much,*

---

[34] The various letters excerpted in this chapter are from the *Daily Telegraph* during the late 1990s.

*but they seem happy to forget about me when they
don't need me. Am I fussing too much or could the
situation be improved?"*

It is no news that today's children and young people worry a good deal about losing friends or their friendships going wrong. And although they talk about it rather less, it is a good bet that adults can also worry about their friendships. There is some evidence indicated by the quotations at the start of this book, that some people do not have any friends. They have no-one to go on holiday with, no-one to visit them when they are ill in hospital, no-one to mourn at their graveside; perhaps no-one they know closely to leave their estate to. Some of these people regret their lack of friends. Another letter from the same paper reads,

*"I am 30 years old and I don't have a clue how to make
friends. If someone so much as smiles at me, I either
follow them around like a lost dog or try to hide my
desperate loneliness by acting indifferent. How do
I make friends?"*

THE LOSS OF WISDOM ABOUT FRIENDSHIP

They worry about friendship because in modern society the word "friendship" is still valued and so is the thing which, for so many people, it incoherently describes; most people want to make friends and want to keep them. They are upset, angry and puzzled when they don't make or keep friends. Their worries may be further exacerbated by the fact that this age which so little understands friendship, makes a cult of it, or at least a cult of what it thinks are friends. There is a highly popular soap opera called "Friends". The media promote the view that glamorous, successful people have friends, rather as they have expensive cars and diamonds. You are a failure if you don't have friends or don't appear publicly with friends.

But it is also true that the supposed solutions of friendship problems have nothing like the airing that solutions to the problems of, for instance, marriage or employment and work get. There are piles of books and a crowd of counsellors queuing up to give advice on the happy marriage or the successful career. But modern society has no established explicit wisdom about friendship. And it may also lack the unspoken wisdom that guided the Eddie generation. To take but one part of explicit wisdom: there is an established knowledge about the ethics of sexual relationships and marriage and another, if more recent, about the ethics of employment and business. Both contain differing views but no-one can doubt that modern society has a lot to say about both. Check the book shops and the libraries or, for that matter, the Internet, and you will find nothing similar about friendship.

At least nothing much written recently. For that is the point; there was a wisdom about friendship. The Greeks and the Romans had it. The early middle ages had it. The Victorians had some of it. And in certain institutions such as the armed services, if not explicit wisdom, then tacit codes about friendship existed until recently. There is a wisdom about friendship but we have lost it.

THE LOSS MATTERS TO SOCIETY AS WELL AS TO INDIVIDUAL FRIENDS

The loss matters most obviously because we value friendship. There are people who are desperately unhappy because they cannot manage their friendships or may not even be able to form them. It is pleasant and enjoyable being with friends and friends can also be useful. At its best friendship gives the friends the opportunities to be pleasant people concerned for each other. But it matters too because, although we obviously still have friendships, there are signs, as I have already said, that they are thinner and feebler than in past times. Certainly modern society's understanding of friendship is thinner than, say, that of the Greeks in the age of Athenian democracy, thinner than in Eddie's times.

If the loss matters to individuals, it also matters to society. It is of the nature of friendship that it is preferential. Having friends means, logically, that there are lots of other people who are not our friends and we care more for the friends than the others. How then can society benefit from friendship? One suggestion is that although we prefer some people to others, the

> "*understanding developed by [friendship] and the mutual criticism involved in it will improve the way friends deal with people outside the [friendship].*"[35]

This is a controversial matter to which we shall return. My own doubt is that only certain kinds of friendship, precisely the kinds that are less common and understood today, can spill over to society's general advantage. All the more reason to be worried about the loss.

Another reason emerged in a discussion with economist Tim Congdon. Those who think free market economies are the best economies usually accept that they require institutions such as the rule of law which are not themselves generated by markets. Free societies need certain institutions and values. Financial markets – Congdon's speciality – require trust. Though some would like to try, it is impossible to regulate for all the fast-moving decisions in such markets. Clients have to trust brokers not to exploit their decisions before those decisions are translated into the broker's action for the client and in many other ways. In Congdon's experience some underdeveloped but regulated economies have had their trade markets very successfully liberalized without much difficulty. But financial markets are more complex. If they are de-regulated without a system of trust being in place, de-regulation is simply a licence for

---

[35] Elizabeth Telfer, "Friendship" in Michael Pakaluk *et al*, *Other selves: philosophers on friendship*, Hackett, New York, 1991, pp 264-5

corruption. And it is not just trust between individuals that is required but social systems of trust whereby there are sanctions for individuals who breach trust, sanctions agreed and administered by society beyond the individuals concerned. In money markets, reputations are important and they involve an ethical-social system. How does one know whom to trust? One needs people with trustworthy characters. How to find a trustworthy person? By asking one's friends whom they know, whom they trust. Friendship supplies a network of trust. It's called "vouching" for someone, and it is a much rarer thing than it used to be.

Another reason why a decline in friendship and the understanding of it matters has already been touched on. It concerns friendship's peculiar relationship with the other institutions which make society work. Society's success depends on an array of stable working institutions such as families, industry and commerce, medicine, law and the professions and defence forces. As we have seen already these have their own wisdoms, rules and codes. Friendships may subvert them but they may also assist them. When, say, a marriage is successful and endures for many years to the happiness and success of all concerned, then there is a temptation to assume that it succeeds because it is a well-made marriage. But what if the heart of that family was not an expertise about relationships or even a deep romantic love between the man and woman? What if what kept them together was their friendship? In other words, friendship may be the ingredient which makes other institutions work. Some other examples may make this clearer. Armies are meant to fight well because of expertise and values of patriotism and service. What if the key to each man's heroism under fire was not love of country but loyalty to the soldier next to him, his comrade, that is, his friend? This argument is common in military history and very explicitly made by Ed Shils and Morris Janowitz about the Wehrmacht in the Second World War.[36]

---

[36] Edward Shils and Morris Janowitz, "Cohesion and disintegration in the Wehrmacht in World War II" in E Shils (ed), *Center and periphery*, University of Chicago Press, Chicago, 1975

Again, large numbers of men and women daily go to work in factories and offices, work they find repetitive and boring. What makes the work bearable and thus the factory or office successful? One ingredient may be the social life, the human contact, the gossip and the humour. Much of this is what might be called sociability but it does not exclude friendships. Friends are made and maintained at work. Yet again, the professions, medicine, law, the church, academe at their best demand of those who study for them, a dedication both as students and as qualified practitioners. That dedication may be fired by a love of the learning or of the patient, client or student. But it may also be fired by respect and emulation of an older doctor, priest or professor the young student has got to know and become friends with.

If friendship is the hidden ingredient which makes so many other social institutions work, it is clear that if it is diluted or misunderstood then what is at risk is not only the pleasure it brings to the friends but the successful working of those institutions. And there are clear signs that this danger is real. For example, recent "reforms" of the armed services have encouraged shorter service contracts and more movement between regiments and other units. Some have even amalgamated such units. This is done in the name of mobility and efficiency. But the separation of men who have learned to serve together, who have become comrades, threatens one of the key motivators of martial virtue.

As regards the family, the modern emphases either on romantic love or sexual satisfaction in marriage and the lack of wisdom and advice about companionship does not bode well for the duration and happiness of many modern marriages. It is crucial that those who want strong families, good schools and brave armies, understand the role friendship plays in them and exploit its possible assistance to these institutions rather than its possible rivalry and subversion of them.

But if the contemporary world is ill at ease with the serious use of "love" and, still more with "virtue", we can still at least understand that what the Old Testament was describing, what David and Jonathan were experiencing, what the Romans and Greeks were exalting, and what Jeremy Taylor so recommended was something profound and demanding. Each of them saw friendship as love and love as a key virtue. Friendship for them was a big thing, so big indeed that it was a foundation in the ideas they taught. And on these ideas, of Judaism, Christianity and classical civilization our own culture is founded. Friendship, then, or at least a certain sort of friendship is one of the foundations of the main blocks of ideas on which our civilization rests.

If we have moved a long way from these foundational sources and no longer mean what they mean when we talk, very less frequently and seriously than they did, about friendship, it is still true that we value friendship. Perhaps we are right to be embarrassed about using the word "love" to explain friendship for today's friendship is so often a lighter affair than that of antiquity. It is a light pleasure, an aid to recreation, a small comfort in times of worry, rather than a fusion of souls in virtue. And rather than being everlasting to and beyond the grave, it may last just until we leave school and go to different universities or jobs, start drinking at the Bell instead of the Bull and meet a new crowd there or switch from tennis to golf and so see rather less of Michael and Anne.

MODERN FRIENDSHIP SEEN THROUGH LETTERS TO AN AGONY AUNT

However if it is not the friendship as it was and perhaps should be, this is not to say modern friendship is worthless. It brings some happiness and is sought. When it is threatened, we start to complain. Consider a few more extracts from letters to a newspaper Agony Aunt.

> *"Dear Anne,*
> *I have returned from a two month trip to Australia with*
> *a close friend. She monopolised conversations, accused*
> *me of religious bigotry and criticised the way I brought*
> *up my children…She is still a very supportive friend and*
> *I value her greatly, but I do feel I should clear the air.*
> *How can I do this?"*

One useful tip given in the sociology books of research methods is that if you want to know what something is, what people expect of it, look closely at what they complain of when it goes wrong. So we learn from this letter to the *Daily Telegraph* that friendship is highly valued, that it is about supporting each other and that it is not to be abused. Abusing friendship includes not respecting other allegiances of friends, such as their religious beliefs or their family. In fact with the family it goes rather further. The writer of this letter is saying that even good friends should not cross boundaries and pronounce on "private" matters. Consider another:

> *"Dear Anne,*
> *We are friends with a couple who are good company,*
> *but the wife is a terrible gossip especially about our*
> *circle of mutual friends…What can we do?"*

Friends, it is clear from this and many similar letters, are expected to be good company, people you enjoy yourself with. They are also expected to share your confidences and not betray them. So, in the letter this chapter started with, we found the writer complaining about being "let down badly" and about her friends forgetting her and forsaking her for someone else who might amuse them better. The friends are bad friends because they lack constancy; they only turn up when they need the writer, when it suits them. Another letter reads:

"I have a close friend who never makes the running in our friendship…I'm always the one to arrange to meet up, and she only ever seems to ring when she's got a problem. I want her to understand that friendship is a two-way thing. What should I do?"

Friendship is a reciprocal relationship. Both parties have obligations. This writer does not say the two friends should have equal obligations but both do have obligations. Importantly, this and many other contemporary writings and discussion about friendship divide friends into types such as close friends, good friends, old friends and, particularly among young people, best, and by implication, not best friends. Thus:

MARRIAGE AND FRIENDSHIP AS RIVALS

"Dear Anne,
My best friend who is twenty has just got engaged to her first serious boyfriend…All her friends have told her they are delighted with the news although I know that secretly they consider him too young and wholly unsuitable…Since I am her best friend, I know I must tell her the truth…Can you tell me how I should broach the subject?"

Best friends clearly have obligations ordinary friends don't have. And once again here is the theme of rival allegiances. We often tend to think of marriage and friendship as good things. But the trouble is that any person usually has plural loyalties to family, friends, country, employer and these can conflict. Today's society is dominated by a romantic and exclusivist notion of marriage, even if the state itself is often short-lived. It's a notion which is extreme and may demand the dumping of old friends on marriage. Divorce and re-marriage are common and re-marriage, even more than first

81

marriage, can see a wholesale clear-out or share-out of friends. Also, while the claim of family and country on one's loyalties are generally and openly recognized, friendship's claims are not so agreed and openly discussed. There's something informal and unpublic about friendship today which can make it hard to maintain when it comes into conflict with other ideals. It may even be illicit in such matters as the awarding of contracts or job appointments.

The most widely listened to and controversial American radio "agony aunt" is a staunch conservative in most things. She takes a sternly moral view of friendship. Again and again she says things like, "She wants you to do THAT and you call her a friend? Friends do not ask friends to do what is immoral." But with her, marriage and children must come absolutely first to the degree that no true friend would want to take you away from your wife/husband and children. Here, friendship suffers because morality itself is feminized. Under cover of keeping vows and being "a good father who works two jobs so mother can stay home with the children" she leaves the working man no time to spend with his buddies. The more affluent man may have more time but certainly not enough for the serious fellowship and conversation that classical friendship entails, certainly few dinners at the club in the old way. Under cover of righting the listing ship of marriage, conservatives of this kind tie the husband to its mast. Thus bound, he is left no time or place for friendship. It is ironic that one traditional value, marriage, when exaggerated can do so much damage to another, friendship.

The agony aunt letter also shows that ordinary, that is, not-best friends, can be made quite quickly. It may take rather longer to become a close or best friend. Some of the research into teenage friendship suggests two to four years. But, especially, young people may describe as a friend someone they met mere days or weeks ago at a party.

FRIENDSHIP, SEPARATION AND DISTANCE

> *"Dear Anne,*
> *I recently started a new job and struck up an immediate*
> *friendship with a colleague."*

This friendship, the letter goes on to explain, subsequently ran into trouble. The friend lets her down cancelling a theatre date at the last minute. Perhaps the friendship will end. The conventional wisdom is that one factor which ends friendship in modern society is increased mobility. As children change schools, later go to different universities and jobs, get married, move about the country in pursuit of their careers, get divorced, re-married and move again, friends get lost. Interestingly, these letters scarcely mention geographical mobility as the cause of broken or lost friendships. What parts friends is the failure of one party to understand or live up to the rules of friendship or tensions between friendship and romance and marriage. One letter even suggests that good friendships survive mobility.

> *"Dear Anne,*
> *Last year I moved to London to be near my children*
> *and also because my friends were dispersing across*
> *the country. My friends promised to keep in touch and*
> *I really thought that this would happen. But now I am*
> *hurt to find out that, for various reasons, no one will*
> *come and visit me…Ironically my older and more*
> *disabled friends tend to be more stalwart and keen*
> *to travel."*

The question of whether friendship can survive physical distance raises a more fundamental one. What happens when friends are parted not by a hundred miles or for a few months but for very long periods or forever? Those who emphasize that friendship crucially involves taking pleasure together, and they include some of the classical writers on pleasure, regard separated friendship as impossible. They may be wrong. The poet Philip Larkin, in his letters[37] often mentioned his preference for writing letters to and receiving them from friends rather than meeting them in person. Perhaps more important than his preference is the fact that friendships such as that with Barbara Pym, fostered by letter, were consolidated when the two met. The separation, far from being an impediment to the friendship, had helped it. Saint Jerome, is often cited as the example of someone who carried on friendship by letter. Other religious writers on friendship go further. Aelred of Rievaulx certainly counts on seeing his friends in the life to come, prays for them and thinks that they pray for their friends still alive. But you do not have to share this particular theological view to think that there is something odd in suggesting that someone ceases to be a friend when you cannot see or hear him. The bond of friendship, love in the David and Jonathan type of friendship, can continue during physical separation. Especially if we allow that friendship may involve unequally requited love, though probably not totally unrequited love – another contentious matter in the friendship literature – then friendship may well endure death. A man does not cease to be his mother's son on her death, why should a friend cease to be a friend?

Separation and distance are of even more concern in the United States not only because of the enormous size of the country but because large parts of the population have always moved about it frequently and comparatively easily. There is a view that this mobility has cost a considerable cultural price in loneliness, isolation and the disruption of sound habits and bonds. Whatever the truth of that, it is remarkable just how many people have kept and do keep in touch. Anecdotal evidence suggests that the generation now in their thirties seem to have closer ties than those of their parents

---

[37] *The selected letters of Philip Larkin, op cit*

especially via new technology. As with the general discussion of friendship in modern society, the question is not whether people say they have friends and stay in touch with them but with the quality of the friendship. We may have to wait to find out if e-mail can be to friendship what the club and pub once were.

The picture of friendship in modern society which emerges from the agony aunt letters is, at first sight, a rather obvious and un-contentious one. We find or "make" friends. We expect to enjoy ourselves with them. We share confidences with them and think they ought not to divulge these to others. Our friends have to pull their weight in the friendship. If they don't do these things, the friendship may end. It may also end when a higher duty to husband or wife or country or some other institution demands. It may be that we should call the relationship the letters discuss companionship rather than friendship, but the intensity of some of the letters suggests an attachment that goes beyond mere recreation even if not to classical friendship.

FRIENDSHIP AS SEEN BY PSYCHOLOGISTS: A LIST OF 'FUNCTIONS'

This picture of modern friendship as largely companionship but with a few residues of true friendship is corroborated by the academic social science research into friendship, especially the twin characteristics of modern friendship, seeking pleasure together and sharing confidences. Friendship is something friends enjoy and, say the psychologists, may be useful to them boosting their esteem and self-understanding. Social scientists are heavily influenced by an interest in what social institutions do, what benefit or function they perform not just for the participants but for society at large. So it is not surprising that we find them listing what friends say they get out of the friendship or what it may contribute to their psychological development or to the functioning of society. The problem here is that the vocabulary of antiquity and its concepts, its very world, is almost ruled out by the concepts and methods of social science. It has no way of studying the fusion of two "souls in unity". Social science is uneasy with the language of love and even uneasier with that of virtue. If it rarely mentions these in its findings on modern friendship it may be because they are rare or because its methods do not help it to identify them. In the latter case we find social science unable to speak about one of the central themes of Christian civilization. Its response to its own muteness and incompetence is either to deny that what it cannot describe exists or to reduce it to phenomena it can describe and in so doing maim and maul it beyond recognition.

It has already been suggested that there is something secret, hidden and unacknowledged about friendships. Just because people do not talk about their loves when given a questionnaire does not mean they do not have them. Nor does it mean that they do. What is most likely is that the very predisposition of social scientists to think and talk about functions and outputs rather than virtue and love is derived from a culture similarly biased.

One of the most published psychologists on friendship, Steve Duck, gives a useful summary of what psychologists have established about contemporary friendships.[38] Friends are expected to be honest and open, to share confidences, spend time with us in activities, repay debts and favours, engage in conversation, not criticize each other in public. Steve Duck then gives a list of the functions of friendship. It gives a sense of belonging and reliable alliance, emotional integration and stability, opportunities for communication about ourselves, physical support and support to our personalities. The well-known book, *How to win friends and influence people*,[39] is a variant on the same theme. It points out how people's personalities, success and income can be enhanced by the use – some might say,

---

[38] Steve Duck, *Friends for life*, Second ed, Harvester Wheatsheaf, 1991

[39] Dale Carnegie, *How to win friends and influence people*, Simon and Schuster, New York, 1936

abuse – of their friends and friendship. Robert Bellah[40] has pointed out how psychologists view friendship as delivering psychic rather than material goods, such as feelings of self-worth. All this, of course is about the uses a friend can derive from "friendship". I put it in "scare" quotation marks because I am far from sure the classical authors would regard this relationship as true friendship.

FRIENDSHIP AND THE SOCIOLOGISTS: A LONG WAY FROM ARISTOTLE

Steve Duck's equivalent in sociology is Graham Allan. Allan also emphasizes the two key characteristics of modern friendship as spending time together in recreation and exchanging and keeping confidences. He sees certain other functions for friendship. It can help in getting jobs, in getting advancement at work, in getting covering for oneself at work when one is ill or elderly, in times of difficulty or emergency. Friendship can give practical support as well as emotional meaning. But Allan is well aware that this, however welcome, is a long way from the classical understanding of friendship.

Aristotle, we have seen, saw the best friendship not just as mutually useful or recreative but as a fusion of virtues, the high point of moral life. A friend, he says, is one who

> *"wishes goods for his friend for his friend's sake"*.[41]

Only the virtuous can be true friends so they will share ideals. They share each other's pains and pleasures. Cicero called friendship,

> *"complete identity of feeling about all things divine and human, as strengthened by mutual goodwill and affection"*.[42]

Duck's and Allan's functions of friendship are about how friendship is useful for me and indeed for you. It is seen as a state which the

---

40 Bellah, *Habits of the heart, op cit* p 134
41 Aristotle, *The ethics of Aristotle, op cit*, p 261
42 Cicero, definition from *Laelius de amicitia* as translated by McGuire, in *Friendship and community*, Cistercian Publications, Kalamazoo, 1988, p xiv

participants get something out of. Aristotle sees it as a virtue practised. Allan is aware that modern friendship is not just about practical functions and is not necessarily instrumental, that is, undertaken for some other purpose. It may be, in the jargon, expressive as well as instrumental, done because we enjoy it for its own sake. However he insists, rightly, I think, that it has little to do with classical friendship, whether in antiquity or more recently. Describing Aristotle's and C S Lewis's view of friendship, he writes that in this,

> "*each gives without thought to cost or reward…from a sociological viewpoint, such a portrayal of friendship is certainly extreme. [It is not] a description of friendships as they routinely occur…[This form of friendship] cannot normally be expected of run-of-the-mill friendships*".[43]

These friendships, real, true and long-lasting, and giving support in times of crisis are few and far between.

What is the nub of the difference between the high, Biblical and classical friendship and most of the relationships called friendships today? Are the two simply different versions of the same thing? It would be silly to deny the value modern people find in modern friendships, the fun they have on games fields, in pubs, talking and laughing together or to deny the sort of emotional support described by Duck or the value of a reasonably secure relationship in which confidences may be told and shared. It is a thing of value. It would also be precipitate to deny that it has some link with the high view of friendship, with what I shall call true friendship. In the brief examination of greetings cards exchanged between friends we see that the cards follow some of the *forms* of the high ideal of friendship. They appear to be about loyalty, shared outlook, confidentiality and support. So what might the relationships be between the two sorts of friendship?

---

[43] This and the following from Graham Allan, *A sociology of friendship and kinship*, Allen and Unwin, London, 1979

Enough has been said to show that I take the gloomy view: modern friendship is in trouble. Many friendships are, to summarize for the moment, lower than the older friendships. But before enlarging on this view, it is important to accept that another, more optimistic view is possible and even plausible. In two of the interviews for this book aspects of it were put very well by two people from the supposed two "sides" of industry: John Monks, General Secretary of the Trades Union Congress and Peter Waterman who has spent a life working for large multinational corporations. Their background is significant because one charge against modern friendship is that it has been driven onto the margins. It is not welcome at work and in public life. Even in leisure it is under siege from the demands of spouse and family and the clubs which once supported it are not what they were.

John Monks makes the point that the old institutions of

> "*family, work, paternalistic employers, big public sector companies, nationalised industries, cradle to grave employment, are waning fast...families are waning fast and I'm aware in the younger generation of a much more important emphasis on friendship and the network*".

It's particularly the case with young women who are, he says, de-liberately trying to replicate an old boys' network in the name of equality. "And they've succeeded" especially in places such as the BBC.

> "*Friendship is doing better than the family, it's doing better than paternalistic frameworks of employment... and the network is the best investment that people make in the future...they fall into bad times, contracts end, jobs end and someone helps you...the informal 'freemasonry' is very commonplace...it's common in*

*London...always has been but it now depends less
on family than before and more on friends."*

More than once, John Monks talks of jobs being

*"passed around groups of friends, a relative for instance
who is a consultant is part of a group of friends who
employ each other as consultants on the basis – it's a
kind of union – that they know each other well...it's a
freemasonry, a support system in an age when the
employer does less".*

And it's not just the professional classes, the law, the universities, it's widespread.

He notes, however, that it is not everywhere. It is not in the Trades Union Congress

*"because of procedures of openness and equal
opportunities policies, but I'm staggered at the number
of places which do [use friendship networks] despite
their formal procedures...There are school dinner ladies
in one London borough. It's a job which is very
convenient and useful if you wish to work hours which
fit a family, you leave when the kids do, you work the
school year...It's a lovely job in your locality and I've
never seen that job advertised...the London working
class pass those jobs about the family, friends and
neighbours. It's very strong."*

And what is sometimes called mentorship, the teaching-learning friendship of a younger and older worker, still happens. It is rare.

*"It was the creature of a homogeneous society but it's
not totally gone."*

Shortly before this interview John Monks had moved house,

> *"The furniture men from Wales shipping our furniture operated like that…There was an old man not doing that much and two lads and the banter between them was pure friendship…what to do with [the furniture] to get it up the stairs…[the old man] occasionally put a shoulder to it and it did move when he pushed it… don't see it often…He was kindly, affectionate, reassuring showing them the right way to do things… It was part of the old apprenticeship system, a mutual respect for age…But it's rare now with nearly half the over fifty year olds not working at all".*

Nor, he argues has friendship gone from leisure.

> *"Watch the young generation…It's a kind of pleasure seeking, they've got money, opportunity, time, not stressed out with small children, mortgage, pressure, jobs and they're students, a larger proportion of students than ever before…it's a kind of epicurean world…drink, sex…it's parties basically…marriage has lost its attraction…children are not to do yet if at all. There's a lot of friendship in young singles…It may not be the idealised form of friendship…It's a network."*

Some of the new friendships are, says Monks, formed much more quickly than the old ones were. In a society in which people move about frequently and move jobs too, you have to learn to make friends fast. That organized "pushy" American style of friendship has a point. You make friends fast or not at all.

That is a point which Peter Waterman agrees with and he shares John Monks' basic optimism. Clubs may not foster the old male-male friendships but that is, on balance, a good thing. The opening up of golf and other clubs has widened the possibilities for friendship. Anyway, for some people the best friend is indeed the wife or husband and single sex clubs, in keeping out one sex, exclude from one's hours of recreation one's best friend. On the work front he does not see it as John Monks does. The days of the big corporation are not over and the big corporation cannot work on a friendship network. It has to have procedures. Appointing friends leads to a conflict of loyalty and interests and in some cases to corruption.

One source for his optimism is new forms of communication. He speaks of a son who rediscovered and reactivated a whole circle of old friends through fax and internet.

It is striking that some of the characteristics mentioned by the psychologists and sociologists, the agony aunt letters and the interviewees in this chapter are those Aristotle would have put in his two lower types of friendship, friendship as mutually useful and friendship as recreation together. With work there is clearly a complex economy today and what is true of a large corporation is not true of the consultancy world and Monks readily admits the rarity of mentorship. What we might notice is that even when friendship networks flourish they are semi-underground. They are certainly not publicly proclaimed. We are not publicly proud of them as the Romans were.

There is one area where at least two interviewees were divided and that is marriage. Peter Waterman is certainly right that some of the best marriages are built on friendship. That apart, it has long been the case that marriage and friendship can be in competition. In another interview, historian Andrew Roberts suggests that with many men working longer hours and with an increasingly child-centred society, friendships are being squeezed out between the demands of work and home. "Men feel, or are made to feel guilty, when they are not at home in the evening with their children". And for him the clubs, whatever they do for married couples, have ceased to be the support they once were for male friends. Nor is he happy with modern communication techniques as aids to friendship. Like many commentators he sees a mutual dependence between conversation and friendship. The question is: do the fax and e-mail promote or kill conversation?

He also mentions another aspect of friendship under threat, that of giving each other advice. And the threat is the growing professional-isation of advice. Where one used to ask family, peers or friends, increasingly one turns to "professional" counsellors and experts. Where business is concerned, friendship and advice are under siege in some quarters for the simple reason that some advice from friends is now illegal. What was once a routine way of choosing investments is now prosecuted as "insider dealing".

However, what does emerge from the optimists' case is that there is still a considerable appetite for forms of friendship and a capacity to create new networks in leisure and some types of business. This would suggest that, if there are elements missing from modern friendship, they are the lack of acceptance of it in public life and, in consequence, the lack of a refined public discussion of friendship and the dislocation of friendship from the life of virtue and love. To the second one might object that true virtuous, loving friendship was only an ideal, rarely or never achieved. Modern friendship, the telephone culture of the greetings cards and the consultants passing around jobs among themselves may be more modest but at least it is practised. According to this view, there is nothing missing from modern friendship; it is simply as much of true friendship as mortals can manage.

Now there is no doubt that true friendship is a daunting ideal, possibly rarely attained. One of the great writers on friendship,

Montaigne seems to suggest it is only attainable by aristocratic classes and then with the greatest difficulty. Moreover he sees it as reclusive, friends battling together against the world, whereas Aristotle sees it as making the world. But if older civilizations failed to achieve true friendships, did they fail in the same way that we fail? I think not. Put bluntly, they may have failed to live up to the ideal, we have changed it. We have removed the heart of friendship which was love in virtue.

THE MORAL COMPONENT FRIENDSHIP SHOULD HAVE AND HAS LARGELY LOST

This is explained well in Robert Bellah's *Habits of the heart*.[44] Speaking of Aristotle and Cicero's view of friendship, "well-known to Americans in colonial and early republican times", he says:

"The traditional idea of friendship had three essential components. Friends must share a common commitment to the good…it is easy for us to understand the components of pleasure and usefulness, but we have difficulty seeing the point of friendship in terms of common moral commitments. For Aristotle and his successors, it was precisely the moral component of friendship that made it the indispensable base of a good society. Those responsible for the early American Republic also understood this. For it is one of the main duties of friendship to help one another become better persons: one must hold up a standard for one's friend and be able to count on a true friend to do likewise. Traditionally, the opposite of a friend is a flatterer, who tells one what one wants to hear and fails to tell one the truth. This profound notion of friendship in which one loves one's friend but, first of all, the good in one's friend, includes the notion of conjugal

---

44 Bellah, *Habits of the heart, op cit* p 115

*friendship as well. The 'unconditional acceptance' that
was supposed to go with true love and friendship did
not mean the abandonment of moral standards, even in
the most intimate of relationships."*

Bellah's mention of flattery is important. Athens of the fourth and
fifth century was the Athens of the democratic ideal and among the
central principles and practices of Athenian democracy was freedom
and frankness of speech. Even after the defeat of democracy by
Philip of Macedon, frankness continued to be valued as a principle
and practice of more personal relationships and was central to the
ideal of friendship. Frankness in speech was the opposite of flattery.
It is interesting in the letters to the agony aunts how several modern
friends seem unable or reluctant to tell their friends the truth
especially about other "friends". De Tocqueville, also writing of
early republican America believed that democracy tended to
universalize flattery.[45] If true, this might explain why friendship has
such a hard time of it in the modern world. And if de Tocqueville is
right then it shows the truly subversive nature of Lloyd George's
remark that "there are no friends at the top".

The modern world tends to think of flattery as a trivial matter. It
may not be a vice at all. If it is one, it is a necessary and minor one.
It was not always so:

> *"There is a place in hell called Malebolge…
> There we heard people moaning…*
>
> *I saw people plunged in excrement
> Which seemed as if it had flowed out of a cesspit.*
>
> *And, while I was searching down there with my eyes,
> I saw one with his head so covered in shit
> You couldn't see whether he was layman or cleric…*

---

[45] De Tocqueville, *Democracy in America, op cit* vol 1, pt 2, ch 7, "On the power that the majority in
America exercises over thought"

And he then, smacking the top of his head:
'So low have I been sunk by the flatteries
Which my tongue was never tired of saying.'" [46]

FRIENDSHIP'S IMPORTANCE IN PUBLIC LIFE

Bellah goes on,

> *"It is also part of the traditional view that friendship*
> *and its virtues are not merely private: they are public,*
> *even political, for a civic order, a 'city', is above all*
> *a network of friends."* [47]

And on this point too the friendship described by Allan, our modern version of friendship, parts company with that of Aristotle. The rupture is also well illustrated in the agony aunt letters. If friendship is no more than a couple of people who play golf and drink coffee together and share their worries about their health and their debts, if friendship is essentially about seeking pleasure together, that excludes it from the world of work, the professions, from politics and academe, from the armed services, from the economy. Yet, as we discussed above, in the past friendship has been thought essential, for instance, in turning soldiers into comrades and making them fight well out of loyalty not so much to their country but to their comrades, and the professions and academe were built on networks of friendships. Doctors and lawyers who trained together maintained loyalties forged in training. Even marriage, the potential rival to friends, was thought to work through friendship, through "comfort".

Allan as a sociologist is concerned with the key institutions of society, government, class, the economy, the family. He notices that his fellow sociologists do not only largely ignore friendship. When they do mention it, they treat it peripherally and do not link it to the world of work or government. Aristotle saw friendship as the basis

---

[46] Dante Alighieri, *The divine comedy*, "Inferno", Canto XVIII, trans C H Sisson, Carcanet, 1980
[47] Bellah, "Reaching out" in *Habits of the heart*, op cit

of society and the state. We have marginalized it from all the institutions that are most important and left it as a leisure pursuit. He saw its heart as based in virtue, we have removed the heart. This is not just to fail at friendship because we are, like all men, weak. We no longer, most of us, have friends in the true sense, nor do we understand what they are.

What is striking about modern friendship is what it is not. It is not to do with the high status things of life, work, the economy, government, church, the professions. It is not seen as useful or essential to their functioning. Insofar as they are institutions of virtue, it is not seen as formative of that virtue. Indeed it is seen as disruptive of these high status institutions. It is not regarded as a virtue but as a comfort. It demands little rather than a lot. It is easily dissoluble. No doubt the high classical ideals of friendship were rarely achieved in practice but they determined the nature if not the total success of actual classical friendships. What has changed is not achievement scores in friendship but the character of the friendship that is being achieved.

Why has this decline occurred? It is time to look at the enemies of friendship.

Overleaf

The Betrayal of Christ Giotto Di Bondone

CHAPTER FIVE

ENEMIES OF FRIENDSHIP:
IN CHRISTIANITY AND THE POLITICS OF RIGHTS

HOW CAN A SPECIAL LOVE BE GIVEN TO FRIENDS IN A RELIGION WHICH COMMANDS ITS FOLLOWERS TO LOVE ALL MEN EQUALLY?

The Christian attitude to friendship is important not only for Christians. Christianity is, after all, one of the main influences on the culture and institutions the modern western world has inherited. So it is of concern to all. But what is it?

The New Dictionary of Christian Theology[48] has a substantial six column entry for "Black Theology", one for "Marxist Theology" and an additional one for Marxism. It has no entry for friendship. Even its entry for "Love" contains no hint of how Christianity views friendship. The 1971 Catholic *Catechism of Christian Doctrine*[49] is scarcely more helpful. It explains that we are commanded by God to love one another "that is, all persons without exception". This "all" is decidedly ominous for friendship. Christians are commanded to love as God loves them, that is fully. So it looks, at first sight, as

---

[48] *The new dictionary of Christian theology*, eds Alan Richardson and John Bowden, SCM Press, London, 1983
[49] *A catechism of Christian doctrine*, Catholic Truth Society, London, 1971

though they are expected to love all men fully and hence equally. Had the Catechism said "any" instead of all, friendship might have stood some chance. But how can a special love, an extra amount of love be justified against Christianity's supposed extreme egalitarianism?

Worse, the Catechism goes on to emphasize that the "all" includes "our enemies". Does the command to love enemies obliterate, as far as we, if not the enemy, are concerned, the distinction between friends and enemies?

A cursory inspection of the pronouncements of modern church leaders, contemporary writings of the church and such like does not show any hostility to friendship. But that is because it does not show any significant mention of it at all. You have to trawl fairly wide and deep to find it discussed at all. You will then discover that a select, tiny group of Classical and New Testament scholars are interested in the extent to which S. Paul was influenced by classical friendship ideas especially in his Epistle to the Phillipians. Biographies of S. Augustine mention his grief at the death of a friend. Some prefer to emphasise his remarks supposedly against friendship which point out that only in God, not human friendship, can trust be securely put. Others show his understanding that God can be loved in close relationships with human others and cite the importance of friendship in his North African Christianity. It is difficult to deny that Aquinas writes approvingly of friendship. So does Jeremy Taylor who more or less equates it with love; but scrupulous linguists may think he mistranslates New Testament meanings of love.

One of the few sustained attempts to assess Christianity's position on friendship is a recent study by Brian McGuire, of how friendship was viewed by the Monastic movement in the early and middle ages.[50] This shows that the subject was thought to have been very

---

50 Brian McGuire, *Friendship and community, op cit*

important although it attracted hostility as well as sympathy. Perhaps more important is how friendship has ceased to be a topic of importance after the first millenium and a half. That means that for the last five hundred years Christianity has largely ignored it. There are exceptions. One often noted is a little book by C S Lewis on *The Four Loves*,[51] one of which is friendship. One less often noticed, for reasons which will become apparent, is a sermon by Cardinal John Henry Newman.[52]

CHRISTIANITY'S RETICENCE AND DIVISION ON FRIENDSHIP

Now Christianity's key virtue is love, and friendship is, as Lewis's title suggests, a love. So this silence is very mysterious. It is the more so because friendship seems to be a widespread human phenomenon – most cultures have friendships even if some individuals don't have any friends – and Christianity is supposed to address the human condition. The recent comparative silence does not mean there is nothing to say though about Christianity and friendship.

McGuire's study shows Old Testament sources emphasising many of the same themes as classical ones, the permanence of friendship, friends helping each other in times of need, the importance of frankness and especially the strength of friendship in a world in which so much else is vanity. In Ecclesiastes there is also the notion that the bond between friends is a common closeness to God. In the New Testament, the message is more mixed. Voluntary friendships are replaced by a command to "follow me" and give up earthly attachments of possessions, home and friendship. And yet Jesus himself had particular friends notably Lazarus and S. John, "the disciple whom Jesus loved".

Despite the comments on Philippians, the Pauline epistles seem to concentrate on the behaviour of the churches, not friendships within them, and the centrality of divine love and human obedience and

---

51 C S Lewis, *The four loves*, Collins Fontana, London, 1963
52 "J H Newman, "Love of relations and friends" in *Selected sermons, prayers and devotions; John Henry Newman*, edited by, J F Thornton and S B Varenne, Vintage Books, New York, 1998

faith. The search for salvation could take turns even more hostile to friendship as in those early ascetics who forsook not just friends but all men and went into the desert to be with God. The only friends in S. Antony's desert life were the angels. McGuire quotes one solitarist,

"Flee from men, stay in your cell, weep for your sins,
do not take pleasure in the conversation of men, and
you will be saved." [53]

Even S. Basil writing his rule for monks of the Eastern church who dwelt together insisted on the importance of community. There were to be no cliques, no particular friendships. He saw something which was to become a persistent reproach against friendships; that they were potentially divisive of a community, subversive and a threat to authority. It should also be noted, however, that he himself was a great friend. His friend S. Gregory Nazianzen is eloquent about their friendship:

"Then, as time went on, we mutually avowed our
affection for one another, and that philosophy was the
object of our zeal. Thenceforth we were all in all to
each other, sharing the same roof, the same table, the
same sentiments, our eyes fixed on one goal, as our
mutual affection grew ever warmer and stronger…envy
was absent…There was a contest between us, not as to
who should have the first place for himself, but how he
could yield it to the other, for each of us regarded the
glory of the other as his own. We seemed to have a
single soul animating two bodies." [54]

AELRED OF RIEVAULX: THROUGH FRIENDS TO GOD

In the western church, if we look at what its leaders *did* as well as what they said about friendship, we see, for instance, that Augustine surrounded himself with and delighted in his Christian friends.

---

[53] McGuire, *Friendship and the monastic community, op cit* p 16
[54] S. Gregory Nazianzen, "On S. Basil The Great, Bishop of Caesarea", in The fathers of the Church; a new translation, vol 22, *Funeral Orations by S. Gregory Nazianzen and S. Ambrose*, published by Fathers of the Church Inc, New York, 1983, pp 39-45

S. Ambrose exalted the joys of friendship and said those joys are good, even godly. God showed us how to be friends with each other. Jerome pioneered the maintenance of friendship through letter writing. Over the next millenium friendship was to wane and return in monastic life. But it reached its height in the life and writings of Aelred of Rievaulx in the twelfth century. Aelred argued that the attraction to other men could be the basis for bringing them closer to God. Though insisting on the evil of homosexuality as an "especially direct way to hell", he believed in

> *"tenderness, affection and touching, and in being open*
> *and talking intimately about one's personal life"* [55]

Beauty, in friends, was worth seeking so long as the pursuit did not lead to sin. He

> *"sought and found God in the impulses of his own heart*
> *and in the experience of men he knew."*

Despite this rich Christian literature on friendship and the endorsement of friendship's importance by that pillar of orthodox Catholic doctrine, S. Thomas Aquinas, after the fifteenth century there is a decline in friendship and a renewal of earlier misgivings about it. S. Francis wrote

> *"the Lord alone, who created the soul is its friend and*
> *no-one else"* [56]

S. Thomas a Kempis warns that friends are a distraction from Christ. S. Francis de Sales warned of the dangers of special friends in religious communities. But the friendship tradition was not entirely dead. McGuire quotes Teresa of Avila,

> *"O Jesus, how wonderful it is when two souls*
> *understand each other. They never lack anything to*
> *say and never grow weary".* [57]

It had, however by then, ceased to be a central Christian concern.

---

[55] McGuire, *Friendship and the monastic community*, op cit p 303
[56] *Ibid* p 413
[57] *Ibid* p 423

C S LEWIS:
FRIENDSHIP AS A SCHOOL FOR VICE AS WELL AS VIRTUE

The two charges against friendship, that it is subversive or distracting from higher loyalties and authorities are made too by Lewis. He wants first to defend friendship. It is neglected today (1960) he complains. He reminds his readers of the great Aristotelian and Ciceronian tradition and emphasises that friendship is indeed a love, and it may be a good love. Friendship is more than companionship and clubbability. It may start from them but it is based on the friends recognizing that they are "are on a common secret road", that they "see the same truth". This can be the moral content identified by Aristotle. Moreover friendship can be useful to society. In an age obsessed with sociological explanations of things, which explain history in terms of structural changes in the economy or culture, Lewis points out that the Romantic movement once was Mr Wordsworth and Mr Coleridge talking incessantly about a secret vision of their own. Communism, Tractarianism, Methodism, the movement against slavery, the Reformation, the Renaissance, might perhaps be said, without much exaggeration to have begun in the same way in friendships.

But then come the problems. What can be the school of virtue can be the school of vice. The shared secret truth can be a lie and an evil lie at that. The delight in company and talk can be exclusive. Friendships can be sets, coteries, gangs, mutual admiration societies. Authority frowns on friendship because

> *"every real friendship is a sort of secession. It may be a rebellion of serious thinkers against accepted clap-trap or of faddists against accepted good sense...it makes good men better and bad men worse."* [58]

It is ambivalent but always subversive.

---

[58] C S Lewis, *The four loves, op cit*, p 75

These worries turn on the definition of friendship. If it is merely a shared secret interest then of course it is ambivalent. But if Lewis really follows the Athenian definition then "bad" friendships are not friendships at all but perversions of friendship, things which have the forms of friendship without the moral content. Of course friendships can go wrong and bad. And Lewis later touches on one way which for Christians is especially worrying. This, unlike the "school for vice", worry is true, almost by definition, for any friendship which forgets God.

Friends, says Lewis, tend to think that they have chosen each other or fallen together by fate. Not so:

> "A secret master of ceremonies has been at work. Christ
> who once said to the disciples, 'Ye have not chosen me,
> but I have chosen you', can truly say to every group of
> Christian friends, 'You have not chosen one another but
> I have chosen you for one another.' The friendship is
> not a reward for our discrimination and good taste in
> finding one another out. It is the instrument by which
> God reveals to each the beauties of all the others...
> At this feast...let us not reckon without our Host".[59]

This is a legitimate worry but only a worry. Again, Lewis goes too far. Friendships, to most orthodox Christians, are not divinely determined. Indeed God is the host, but He does not compel the guests to come to the feast. In forming friendships we do discriminate and exercise taste and act freely. In good friendships, in true friendships as in any other good action, we do so by co-operating with the divine intention – but operating nevertheless.

What C S Lewis says about friendships can be said about families or even churches. They too can become cliques. They can become exclusive, wrapped up in themselves, oblivious, even subversive of

---

[59] *Ibid*, p 83

divine authority. But no-one in Christian history ignores them and attacks them in the way friendship has been ignored and attacked. Friendships can be perverted from their true nature, from the best, but that does not explain why they as a form of human association have been singled out for criticism and, even worse, silence.

The point can be made more constructively. If friendship is a powerful force for virtue and vice and if it is a good thing which can be perverted into a bad thing, then why has not the church, over two thousand years, built up a sophisticated wisdom on how to distinguish good and bad friendship, on how it is perverted. There is a huge body of Christian ethics on the family, why not on friendship? Whatever side one takes in the dispute about friendship, the important point is that there is a dispute. Christianity is not agreed, has not agreed during its entire history what it thinks about particular friendships. If friendship is in trouble today, the silence and confusion of Christianity is at least partly responsible for it.

SUBVERSION OF AUTHORITY NOT THE MAIN CHARGE AGAINST FRIENDSHIP

The main objection to particular friendship today is not primarily on the grounds that it is subversive. It is that it is particular. In a nutshell, Christians are called to love all men, not to choose a few to love who are their friends. It is of the essence of friendship that it is preferential: I become friends with a few people and love them more than others, love those others less than my friends. Ethics today, including Christian ethics, has strong universalistic tendencies. It emphasizes each person's obligations to all men regardless of race, sex or age, regardless of whether they are friends or enemies. It may even go so far as to imply, as we have seen, that we should love all men *equally*.

THE PARABLE OF THE GOOD SAMARITAN:
LOVING ALL MEN, NOT JUST ONE'S FRIENDS

The most popular alleged Biblical justification for this is the parable of the Good Samaritan. A lawyer agrees with Christ that he has an obligation to love his neighbour and asks who his neighbour is. Christ replies with the story of a man who is robbed and left for dead by the roadside. The person who eventually helps him is not a man of his own race, a Jew, but a Samaritan, a race looked down on by the Jews. The first point of the parable is that need, not race, is the essential factor in the obligations of charity. We should love and help anyone in need regardless of race, age, sex, religion. Many commentators add a rather different lesson that all men are our neighbours. We should love as God loves and He loves all men.

This is more questionable. Is the lawyer being told to love all men or any man he finds himself with, who is in need? There is a great deal of difference. The first is universalistic; the second particular. In the second case we are to love, as it were, those near to us. It is true, of course, that Christians are to try to love as God does. But they are not to imagine themselves gods. He can love all men. We cannot do so; or at least we cannot love and help all men in the world at the same time.

There are other reasons not to identify Christianity too much with ethical universalism. The Church may have regrettably little to say about friends but it has a lot to say about families. One of the Ten Commandments exhorts us to put our father and mother before other men in honour. Christ himself showed an especial love for His mother. It would be the most bizarre ethical system which did not urge men to love their parents, spouses, children more than someone else's parents, spouses and children. The Church's marriage service does indeed urge special duties of love with regard to the last three. That means we love other people's parents less than our own.

There is no getting away from it. And if we are to love our families more than other men's, why not our friends?

NEWMAN: THE CALL TO LOVE A FEW MEN IN PRACTICE RATHER THAN ALL MEN IN THEORY

John Henry, Cardinal Newman is a lone voice acknowledging the implications of this. In fact he does not only acknowledge them, he launches into a tirade of condemnation and mockery of those who think otherwise. It comes in a sermon preached on the feast of S. John the Evangelist.[60] He notes that John was one of the three or four disciples, along with Peter, Andrew and James who were closest to Christ. S. John, the "disciple whom Jesus loved" was, then, Christ's "bosom friend". He was "the private and intimate friend". He goes on:

> *"It might be supposed that the Son of God Most High*
> *could not have loved one man more than another;*
> *or again, if so, that He would not have had only one*
> *friend, but, as being All-holy, He would have loved*
> *all men more or less, in proportion to their holiness.*
> *Yet we find our Saviour had a private friend...*
> *[Thus] there is nothing contrary to the spirit of the*
> *Gospel, nothing inconsistent with the fullness of*
> *Christian love, in having our affections directed in*
> *an especial way towards certain objects, towards*
> *those whom the circumstances of our past life, or*
> *some peculiarities of character, have endeared us."*

Then comes the tirade:

> *"There have been men before now, who have supposed*
> *Christian love was so diffusive as not to admit of*
> *concentration upon individuals; so that we ought*
> *to love all men equally. And many there are, who...*

---

60 J H Newman, "Love of relations and friends", *op cit*

consider that the love of many is superior to the love of one or two; and neglect the charities of private life, while busy in the schemes of an expansive benevolence...Now I shall maintain here, in opposition to such notions of Christian love, and with our Saviour's pattern before me, that the best preparation for loving the world at large, and loving it duly and wisely, is to cultivate an intimate friendship and affection towards those who are immediately about us...

How absurd it is when writers...talk magnificently about loving the whole human race with a comprehensive affection, of being friends of all mankind...this is not to love men, it is but to talk of love. The real love of man must depend on practice... It is obviously impossible to love all men in any strict and true sense. What is meant by loving all men, is to feel well-disposed to all men, to be ready to assist them, and to act towards those who come our way, as if we loved them. We cannot love those about whom we know nothing; except indeed we view them in Christ, as the objects of his Atonement, that is, rather in faith than love. And love, besides, is a habit, and cannot be attained without actual practice, which on so large a scale is impossible...

A man, who would fain begin by a general love of all men, necessarily puts them all on a level, and instead of being cautious, prudent and sympathising in his benevolence, is hasty and rude; does harm, perhaps, when he means to do good, discourages the virtuous and well-meaning and wounds the feelings of the gentle.

Men of ambitious and ardent minds, for example,
desirous of doing good on a large scale, are especially
exposed to the temptation of sacrificing individual to
the general good in their plans of charity. Ill-instructed
men, who have strong abstract notions about the
necessity of showing generosity and candour towards
opponents, often forget to take any thought for those
associated with themselves; and commence their
(so-called) liberal treatment of their enemies by an
unkind desertion of their friends...private virtue is
the only sure foundation of public virtue."

Newman recalls that

"the Ancients made friendship a virtue. In a Christian
view, it is not quite this; but it is often accidentally a
special test of our virtue. [It may well be] a symbol of
divine grace for there is something of the nature of
virtue in the very notion of constancy [in friendship]".

It is Newman too who sees it is an attribute of God – not man – to combine love of all and love of one man harmoniously:

"Thou art careful and tender to each of the beings Thou
hast created, as if it were the only one in the whole
world. For Thou canst see everyone of them at once,
and Thou lovest every one in this mortal life, and
pursuest every one by itself...as if Thou wast waiting on
it and ministering to it for its own sake".[61]

But Newman stands more or less alone. In his life time he was ridiculed for such "unmanly" feelings; famously by Charles Kingsley; viciously by many others. That his understanding of friendship should be derided as part of a wider suspicion of the effeminate, celibate and precious tells us more about the society than

---

[61] J H Newman, "The providence of God" in *Meditations and devotions by John Henry Newman*, Burns and Oates, London, 1964, p 92

it does about Newman. He is said to have had a great influence on the modern church. But that is not true of his doctrine of friendship. Indeed with the modern church's obsessions with universal human rights and social and political justice for all men, it has consistently taken the side of "expansive benevolence" and ignored the love of friends "immediately about us".

THE BETRAYAL OF FRIENDSHIP IN THE NEW TESTAMENT: JUDAS AND PETER

It would be precipitate, however, to leave the consideration of Christianity and friendship without mention of one little matter. John Greenwood, when discussing in an interview the suggestion that the Bible has little to say about friendship, made a general point: Abraham, Moses, the patriarchs and the prophets were considered friends of God and there is a continuing theme in Old and New Testament of intimacy with God. It was while talking round this point that we stumbled on the little matter. Take any Greek or Roman, any "high" concept of friendship or even take a modern shallow notion of friendship and ask what is the essential virtue that goes with it and it is surely loyalty. We stand by our friends, we don't let them down. What is the vice which is the opposite of loyalty? It is obviously treachery and betrayal. Now it may be that the word "friend" occurs rarely in the Bible but the most solemn moment of the New Testament, the moment that sets off the events that make the Christian religion – that is the events of the Passion, Crucifixion and Resurrection – is the moment when Judas betrays Christ.

What is the betrayal a betrayal of? Is it a betrayal of God and the teachings of Jesus? Perhaps, but not centrally. It is a betrayal of Christ who was Judas' friend. Judas has been with Christ for perhaps three years. He has been his friend and he has been trusted with the funds of the disciples and Jesus. He has shared in their joys

111

and troubles, in their conversations, in their knowledge. Indeed he uses his knowledge of Christ and disciples' movements to betray Him and them in the Garden of Gethsemane. He uses the sign of friendship, the kiss, to betray his friend. The gesture of love is perverted into treachery. And the Authorized Version records that the first word Jesus said to him at that kiss was "friend": "Friend, do that for which thou art come."[62]

The horror of that moment is a horror of friendship betrayed. We are clearly meant to be shocked by S. Matthew's account and what is shocking is the betrayal of a friend. And the value, the extent of the evil of that betrayal is surely witness to the value, the extent of virtue put by the New Testament on friendship. And the betrayal becomes yet more awful when set in context. The friend betrayed to be killed the next day was the same friend who only hours earlier has said to the disciples:

> *"greater love than this no man hath, that a man*
> *lay down his life for his friends…I have called*
> *you friends."*[63]

And the friend so soon to be betrayed has dipped bread in a bowl and handed it to Judas. And Judas, knowing that to eat bread with another was the sign of security, has taken it and eaten it, then gone out and betrayed Him.

And if that is not enough for those who say they cannot find anything about friendship in the Scriptures, see what happens next. But first remember back three years. When Jesus called the disciples, he took a special walk along the Jordan with Peter, John and Andrew. They, among the disciples were his special friends. And it is made clear that of them, Peter was considered most special of all. Peter was "the Rock". Soon after the betrayal by Judas in the Garden of Gethsemane, the "Rock" fled, with the rest of Jesus' friends. He fled. But he was recognized by a servant-maid at the gate of

---

[62] S. Matthew: ch26, v50 Authorized version of *The Bible*
[63] S. John's Gospel: ch15, vv13-14 Authorized version of *The Bible*

Caiphas. She asks him if he is not one of the disciples, Jesus' friends, and he denies it, not once but three times. He who once said, "Thou art the Christ, the Son of the living God" now says, "I know not the man". Then the procession that was bearing Jesus away passes by Peter and the evangelist records simply, "And the Lord turning looked on Peter". Jesus had heard what Peter had said and the friend denied forgave the friend who had denied Him. Then Peter "began to weep".[64] There is a tradition that Peter wept every day till his death so that his face was lined by the passage of grief and remorse. And the essence of that remorse is for what he had done to his friend. This scarcely suggests there is no endorsement of friendship in the New Testament.

When Dante comes to describe the "emperor of the kingdom of pain" in hell we learn he has three faces.

> "With six eyes he wept, and down three chins
> Dripped tears and dribble, mixed with blood.
>
> In each mouth he was chewing with his teeth
> A sinner, as if pounding him with spikes
> So that he kept the three of them in torment.
>
> For the one who was in front, the biting was nothing
> Compared with the clawing, so that at times his spine
> Was left stripped of every scrap of skin.
>
> 'That soul there, which has the worst punishment,
> Is Judas Iscariot', my master said,
> 'With his head inside, and kicking his legs.'
>
> Of the two other, who hang upside down,
> The one who hangs from the black face is Brutus;
> See how he twists and says not a word;
>
> And the other is Cassius. Whose body looks so heavy."[65]

---

64 S. Luke: ch22, v60 Authorized version of *The Bible*
65 Dante Alighieri, *The divine comedy, op cit* Canto XXIV

Here is Judas who betrayed his master and his friend Jesus; Brutus who betrayed his emperor and his friend, Caesar. And what place is reserved for these betrayers of friends? It is they, not gluttons, heretics or even thieves who are at the heart of hell.

CONTEMPORARY SECULAR PHILOSOPHY ALSO HOSTILE TO FRIENDSHIP

The hostility to friendship found in some strands of Christianity is also found in secular philosophies of today. And for some similar reasons. Much secular moral philosophy is founded on the idea that the moral is closely connected with the impartial and the universalizable. Pakaluk in a reader on friendship explains it like this:

> "*A reason for action is* universalizable *if it can be converted into a general law that ought to be binding on all rational agents in similar circumstances. For example a person on a crowded beach has a reason to turn down the volume on his radio, and his reason for doing so might be thought to be universalizable in the sense that the other beach goers, who are in a relevantly similar situation, would have the same reason to turn their radios down as well. In such cases it is natural for the agent to view himself as one among many equal persons and to see his action as bound by a pattern of lawfulness that binds everyone equally. But the reasons that friends have for doing good for each other seem to have a different character. First, friends regard each other not simply as one among many but as unique individuals to whom they are related in ways they are not related to humanity at large. Second, because of their familiarity and shared experiences, they have reasons for acting that seem unavailable to non-friends. And third, those reasons seem*

*not to be straightforwardly universalizable. I might
have a reason to give my friend the last crust of bread
that no non-friend, no mere rational agent would have.
To inquire whether a reason for action is universalizable
is, in effect, to pose the question: "What if everyone
acted like that?" But the question seems odd and even
irrelevant when put in the mouth of a friend deciding
how to act towards his friend."*[66]

Pakaluk goes on to stress a second aspect of much contemporary morality. This is a certain impartiality or disinterestness. Moral actions should be unbiased, not motivated by personal material or emotional interest, by hate, envy or indeed love. Friendship, however, is partial. It is a sort of love. It is also preferential. John, Mary and Peter are my friends. Which means that Jerry, Bob, Gill and the rest of the world known to me are not. And among my friends, John is my best friend. According to the rules even of modern shallow friendship I have obligations to John that I don't have to Bob. I put him before Bob.[67]

Pakaluk also points to another aspect of contemporary philosophy, the defining of the good as the maximisation of welfare. Good actions are those which produce the greatest happiness or other benefit for the greatest number. But friends are not interested in the greatest number. They do not act towards each other with a view to helping others. In one sense they do not seek any consequences. The friendship is an end in itself.

MODERN EMPHASIS ON UNIVERSAL RIGHTS AND EQUALITY ARE AGAINST THE PREFERENTIAL CHARACTER OF FRIENDSHIP

Thus several key ideas of contemporary moral philosophy are not only at odds with friendship; they would seem to rule it out as a moral affair, or at least as an affair of justice. And when we look

[66] M Pakaluk, "Introduction", *Other selves: philosophers on friendship, op cit*
[67] Further discussion on these ideas is in Lawrence Blum, *Friendship, altruism and morality*, Routledge, Kegan & Paul, London, 1980, pp 87-105

at contemporary political creeds, the picture is worse. Two related ethical-political dogmas reign in today's world, that of egalitarianism – we should treat all equally – and that of universal rights – that all human beings have claims on others. But friends care nothing for rights in making friendships or in doing things for friends they do not do for others. And friendship is manifestly not even anti-egalitarian.

It may be there are ways of reconciling friendship with the tenets of contemporary philosophy and politics. Robert Grant argues that universalism is not so much unsatisfactory as insufficient. Morality needs to be built on sympathy, virtue and piety as well as reason.[68] But the reconciliation is not an easy task. And it is complicated because friendship would seem to have a place, indeed an unfashionable place, in the scheme of political philosophy. The sort of considerations discussed above about equality, rights and a certain sort of justice are the pre-occupations of socialists. Liberals in the classical English sense also have certain key objectives and they centre on liberty. The high ideal for many conservatives is social order. Put another way, what they fear is chaos and violence. They value an orderly society where men may go about their chosen business governed by the rule of law and by custom and morality. They do not imagine that this order can be planned. The orderly society is one which has organically evolved. Whatever the various merits of these political creeds, it is fairly obvious where friendship is likely to fit. It receives some succour from liberalism because friendship is voluntary and chosen, so it needs liberty. But it is even closer to conservatism because like it, friendship is organic. Even more clearly the agenda of modern socialism, universal rights and egalitarianism, has nothing to offer friendship; it may even be opposed to it and replace it with its own ideas of fraternité or compulsory universal friendship and comradeship. Organic conservatism is not a popular ideology in the modern world, though

---

[68] Robert Grant, ""The meaning of liberalism", *op cit*, pp 77-8

it does fit the facts of many ordinary lives. And thus friendship finds itself ignored, misunderstood or even opposed by contemporary political thinking.

Does it matter that friendship is ignored or dismissed by dominant contemporary ideas? Indeed it does. It might not matter if these ideas were confined to the university. But they increasingly influence public policy and business. In the contemporary passion for "ethical" politics and "ethical" business practices, friendship is increasingly defined as a danger. There are all sorts of egalitarianism but their differences do not concern us here. At root, egalitarianism defines moral behaviour to others as impartial and equal. Of course it allows us to treat people differently but only some sorts of difference are acceptable. We treat those who steal from us differently from those who do not. But even then, we should treat all who steal to the same extent in the same way. Friendship offends partly because it is partial; it puts some before others; and partly because the grounds on which it does so are not those countenanced by egalitarianism. When I make a friend I choose him, he chooses me and we make our friendship according to our moral and affective dispositions. Not only do we take no notice at all of egalitarian codes but in putting each other first we put others second, last or nowhere at all. The words associated with friendship, partiality, particularism are sins in the egalitarian book.

It is possible that a more sophisticated analysis might object to the extreme opposition of friendship and egalitarianism. Might not, as Cardinal Newman suggests, loving someone be a preparation for loving everyone? Might not it be an instance of loving everyone? Could it be that the choice of a friend rests on the same virtues that are good for society in general? Possibly. But even then friendships are not made with that general good in mind. The whole way of acting that is friendship is a million miles from the way of thinking, political action and regulation that is egalitarianism and their vocabularies are almost entirely distinct from each other. From the point of view of modern ethics, modern political ideology and modern Christianity, friendship is about as good and about as interesting as tribalism. And when we get to the codes of political correctness derived from these modern ethics, politics and religion, friendship, putting one before another on the basis of personal disposition, is increasingly "unacceptable" especially if let loose in the world of work and reward.

Overleaf

The Letter of Introduction Sir David Wilkie

CHAPTER SIX

THREATS TO FRIENDSHIP AT WORK:
SHOULD I GIVE A JOB TO MY FRIEND?

FRIENDSHIP AND THE CULT OF TRANSPARENCY

Over the last half century, several of the ideas about rights and equality mentioned in the last chapter have become prominent in business ethics. And business ethics has gone from being an abstract set of ideas to an actual interference, sometimes in the case of "insider dealing" as it is known in the UK and "insider trading" in the USA, and "non-discrimination" a legal requirement in the conduct of actual businesses. In the UK, the Companies Act, the Financial Services Act, UK and Euro regulations of insider dealing, the requirements of the various UK and European equal opportunity and human rights statutes and government bodies together with reports such as the Cadbury Report now affect how the daily dealings of business are done. In the USA, the Equal Employment Opportunity Commission, the Occupational Health and Safety Administration and the Americans with Disabilities Act reach into every aspect of the lives of businesses, schools, the private practices of law and medicine and even churches. These federal acts and agencies are in addition to local regulations made pursuant of them and state regulations. In running even the smallest business one is forbidden to do many things that seem quite natural. For example, if, in interviewing prospective employees one asks a person's age or number of children – simply wondering how much a mother might be off work for childhood illnesses – one is quite likely to be open to an action for discrimination.

There is now a huge literature on what is and what is not ethical when hiring, promoting and firing personnel, when awarding contracts to suppliers, when using or disclosing non-public material information (especially "insider dealing"), when advising as a non-executive director. The businesses which this business ethics seeks to regulate were once major sites of friendship. Look at the origin of many of the great banks such as Morgans and you see they grew from the informal associations of men who knew each other as friends or acquaintances. Business is based on trust. It is an exchange based on the management of risk and trust is the best and fastest way of managing risk. To trust someone, you have to know him and acquaintance and friendship are modes of knowing people. A lawyer, explains Gary Shugg, an investment company director who previously practiced as a lawyer, when asked to prepare a deal worth millions used to accept the work knowing that he would be paid as a matter of trust. Today he requires payment "up front". Credit was based on friendship or at least acquaintanceship, knowing the borrower and knowing his friends in front of whom he would be shamed if he defaulted. Businesses were started not by "institutions" but by a collection of friends putting money in, risking their money in friendship. Now it is done through institutions which are slower and more cumbersome, especially for the crucial first half million pounds. And credit is done on points registered by computer programmes. Some, the Bengalis, the Jews, the overseas Chinese still use friendship and it accounts for no small part of their success.

So central was friendship in business that various institutions in the financial market (the "City of London"), university senior common rooms and medical schools used to be referred to as "clubs". Those who disliked them called them "old boys' networks". What happens when the new ideas about transparency and proceduralism and the codes and regulations based on them meet habits established by friendships and "clubs" on the site of business?

Friendship, we have seen, is preferential. Turn that term round and it can quickly become "excluding". Friendship advantages some and excludes others. Friendship, if not secret, contains a mass of private understandings. That means non-friends might be "denied" information. And friendship is informal. From Aristotle on, analysts of friendship use the word "grow" to describe the development of friendship. It is not planned and set up formally. Though Macbeth is far from a good friend, he and his fellow characters in that play know all about the language of growth in friendship:

> "KING (to Macbeth): Welcome hither.
> I have begun to plant thee and will labour
> To make thee full of growing. Noble Banquo,
> That has no less deserved nor must be known
> No less to have done so, let me enfold thee
> And hold thee to my heart.
> BANQUO: There if I grow,
> The harvest is your own."[69]

Such nurtured relationships do not fit timeless, abstract procedures. You do not have to have a very incisive mind to see that the arrival of a ethics code which relies heavily on universalistic, open, non-discriminatory, written procedures might well find itself in conflict in business milieux with habits and associations which have grown organically and are run on informal, spontaneous, evolved lines. Friendship is key among them.

---

[69] William Shakespeare, *Macbeth*, I, iv, Penguin, London, 1956

The clash between the two has never really come to a head. Some financial analysts such as David Lascelles think friendship is still at the heart of financial business in the UK but has gone underground. Though he also notes that the forms of association where friendship most flourished, such as partnerships, have given way to larger corporations. Businessman Jamie Borwick makes a similar point about family companies and plcs. For its part, the business ethics movement has never, to my knowledge condemned friendship in business directly. Most of the major reports do not even mention it. But the clash of cultures is pretty clear.

Most business ethics codes are meritocratic and emphasize transparency. Selection, advancement and contract should be by merit, relevant merit for the purpose rather than who-knows-who. Transparency means that everything that a public institution, civil service, local government, the police, schools and a publicly quoted company do, should be open, visible, accountable. For instance when someone is appointed to a job vacancy the criteria should be laid down, the person appointed be interviewed and selected according to the written criteria, procedures followed and equality of opportunity assured and seen to be assured. The whole process should be open to inspection by those who have a right to see it. In such a firm or government service, friendship is at least a potential enemy. Not only is it preferential but it is confidential. It is an underground system of undeclared, unregistered loyalties in which secrets are passed and held.

WORK-FRIENDS AND HOME-FRIENDS

Worse, at least at one time, friendships straddled home and work and past and present. A person might introduce those whom he met at home, at golf, at dinner, in the past at school, university or the armed services to his firm or profession – and vice versa. Advantages and obligations acquired in one place or at one time might seep into other places and times. And so might information. What A knew about B from mutual friends might inform his business treatment about B. And at least some of the traditional thinking about friendship would even applaud this. Cicero thought it quite proper that friendships should result in material advantage, though he made it clear that an association entered into for material advantage was no friendship.

The modern tendency is to view the slippage of advantages and obligations from home and leisure to work as dangerous. The assumption is that obligations felt towards friends at home will result in inappropriate favours being awarded at work. On the contrary, true friendship has standards which are more exacting than routine business ethics. Fear for loss of reputation at home, among friends, is a sharper goad to good business practice than abstract business ethics codes. Censure or even sacking may be far less effective sanctions than loss of reputation, friends and social isolation. What used to be called "loss of one's name" was some-thing to be feared. If it did happen "retrieving one's name" was crucial to reestablishing oneself in business. And for these sanctions and incentives of reputation to work, there has to be a connection between work and home.

I mentioned in earlier chapters that friendship is increasingly being unacknowledged, even disapproved of, in the world at work. This does not mean that it does not exist in the place of work. People make friends and keep friendships going in offices and factories. In fact such sociability often keeps people working and working well at otherwise dull or poorly rewarded jobs. Friendship exists at the place of work but it and friends have no rights, no acknowledged claims there. And the friends of home certainly have no such claims there. Indeed Jamie Borwick and others in business suggested that as far as London and other major cities are concerned, distance and the time required to cover it due to increased traffic meant that businessmen increasingly had two fairly distinct sets of friends, in business, and at home.

GIVING A JOB TO A FRIEND

The new drive for transparency is a drive against friendship precisely because, while friendships are maintained at work, it cannot admit the propriety of their preferential private and informal character in what it defines as business spheres. Consider an example. I am an employer. I have to make an appointment. I have ten applicants. Eight I have never met. Two, I know. I know the son of a cousin very well. Another I have met and liked and she is the friend of a friend who vouches for her strongly, if a little vaguely. The son of my cousin I know to be lazy and dishonest. The one known through a mutual friend I understand to be clever, decent, hardworking and just right for the job. Indeed I know more about her than about any of the eight. About them I only know what application forms and bland references reveal. One reason the references are bland is that those who write them are also increasingly mindful not to say anything for which they cannot produce evidence, for they too are governed by universalistic, bureaucratic, transparent and egalitarian codes. It is not unknown today for a referee who is also a friend of the employer to telephone to have "a word in your ear", off-the-record, and correct, as it were, the written reference; this subversion of references is normal practice in American academic life where transparency and blandness have combined to make them useless. Perhaps most important of all, the mutual friend is a proper friend, the sort who would not let me down, whose shared morality in friendship means that he would not abuse the friendship to seek to advance his friend unless she deserved it.

According to commonsense and traditional wisdom, I might well not even interview the son of my cousin. There is nothing against him on the application form but I know plenty from less formal sources. And perhaps I should appoint the person known to my friend without wasting the time and unnecessarily raising the hopes of the other eight candidates. I have adequate and reliable information about the candidate recommended by the mutual friend and that friend is willing to go out on a limb to support her. That is, his friendship is a guarantee. If she turns out to be a failure, my friend will suffer at least acute embarrassment, possibly loss of my friendship. Anyway, I know him better than I know the referees. Judged solely by the aim of finding someone who will do the job successfully, I might well choose the woman known via friendship. City businessman Gary Shugg has no doubts:

> *"I would always give a job to a friend,*
> *I know more about them".*

In many of today's companies, government offices, universities and hospitals it would be inconceivable to do so. For the issue is not finding the right person for the job but being fair to all the applicants and treating them equally. If I appoint the friend of the friend, and am discovered doing so by the commissars of transparency, I might well lose my job. The move towards transparency is said to be efficient. By denying a crucial role to the important information derived from friendship and by scorning notions of trust, it is actually inefficient. It is, however, according to fashionable definitions of the term, just.

THE OLD BOY NETWORK

In some other less progressive institutions, or ones such as family firms and partnerships less fearful of state enforced egalitarianism and transparency, to appoint the friend might be accepted but I would have to make the grounds very explicit. Elaine Sternberg, in an interview and in her book, *Just business*[70] has no truck with

---

[70] Elaine Sternberg, *Just business: business ethics in action*, second edition, Oxford University Press, Oxford, 2000; first edition, Little, Brown and Co, London, 1994; Warner paperback, London, 1995

politically-correct thinking and is much more ethically robust than the run of business ethicists. Of course I may appoint the friend of the friend. What matters is that she should have the functional abilities and character to do her job well. In public business corporations, the test is whether she is the candidate most likely to enhance the long-term shareholder value which all the directors, including the appointing director, have an ethical fiduciary duty to promote. Indeed I may even use the mutual friend's recommendation.

> *"There is nothing wrong in an "old boy network" as such: it is natural and valuable for mutual support systems to exist among those with much in common. Moreover, such networks can be extremely useful to business. They can constitute a reliable source of employees who are relatively easy to evaluate; their informal social sanctions can be productively used to promote business objectives…The only occasion when an "old boy network" should provoke concern is if it is regarded as the sole acceptable source of recruits."*[71]

Dr Sternberg's advice, however, is both brave and unusual. But even she adds a rider. In appointing the friend, I should make my grounds very explicit. The friend's recommendation will be a part of the girl's application, as available to scrutiny as the rest of it; the number and identity of the persons to whom it would be disclosed would vary with the circumstances. But I asked Elaine Sternberg, "what if I can't be very explicit?" I have already mentioned that the mutual friend's recommendation though unequivocal was a trifle vague. And it's no use badgering him for details, I've known him for years, his judgment always was first class but his memory lousy. Friendship and its knowledge is often "vague", inexplicit and informally recorded and may not yield a list of reasons of the sort that someone outside the friendship would recognize. One of the reasons why

---

[71] *Ibid* pp 135-6

friendship is so good for decisions is that it is a short cut. One is making a decision not on a mass of new evidence, a pile of ten-page application forms but on the basis of a one line comment from another person who has always made reliable decisions and recommendations. The reliability turns not on the amount of evidence and the details but on *who* the recommender is – a friend. This otherwise advantageous aspect means the recommendation will often not be able to explain itself.

She replies that what needs to be made explicit is the director's relationship of friendship with the recommender, and the fact that the relationship is the basis of his confidence in the content of the recommendation; that can be done regardless of the degree of detail contained in the recommendation. Unless the appointing director is wholly abdicating his responsibility, however, by delegating it uncritically to the friend (which would be a violation of his duties to the corporation) then, especially since the friend has a poor memory, it would be prudent at the very least to interview the girl and probably to subject her to the same tests as the other candidates: one wants to be sure for example that the friend has not confused her with someone else. Other things being equal, she will get the job; if she is as good as the recommendation claims, she will do very well on the interview and at the tests and she will also presumably have a much better reference. Doing this may also satisfy regulatory requirements and provide a defence against disappointed, litigious candidates.

Dr Sternberg is persuasive. My only reservation is what should happen when the results of informal, friendly recommendation clash with those of formal tests and interviews. And there is one further difficulty – and on this too I part company with Elaine Sternberg. The business ethicists are largely concerned with what constitutes good behaviour for the business. But I also have obligations to my friend. Not to take seriously, perhaps not to accept a sound re-commendation from him is a slight to our friendship – though he would never take it as such. She replies that it is no slight. Even if I have asked a friend for advice, if that advice proves incompatible with other constraints which he may or may not have known about when giving his advice, then the advice should not be followed. It might be courteous to explain to the friend why his suggestion has not been accepted, but both friends should understand that what is owed to the friend is thanks not uncritical acceptance.

That is probably right, but I still have the feeling that a slight might have been done to friendship if not to the friend. Of course, I should think as clearly as possible about the choice I have. But no amount of clarity can disguise the fact that there could be a clash of cultures here. Informal ethical procedures, as Dr Sternberg agrees, clash with conventional, (largely unethical) business ethics which have adopted the legalistic language of procedures, non-discrimination, trans-parency and formality.

SHOULD I TIP OFF MY FRIENDS ABOUT SHARES?

We can pursue this culture clash through a consideration of insider dealing and friendship. Business ethicists are divided over insider dealing. A short definition is "the buying or selling of securities on the basis of material, non-public information".[72] The first point to make is that before Big Bang, that is, only a short time ago, almost all dealing was insider dealing. Dealing was done by being given information by friends. Several of my interviewees reported that getting three tips a week was usual. One said that everyone did it; actually what he said was, "everyone does it".

There are two worries expressed about it. The first comes from a heightened concern, fuelled by egalitarianism about those allegedly not being treated equally by this either in terms of access or

---

[72] Jennifer Moore, "What is really unethical about insider trading?" in A R Prindl and Bimal Prodhan (eds), *The ACT guide to ethical conflicts in finance*, Blackwell, 1994

information. But there are plenty of cases where participants in markets have different levels of access or information. The more serious objection is when insider dealing essentially means the dealer is betraying his duty to his shareholders, lying or stealing information. This sort of insider dealing is clearly wrong.

More to the point, it is wrong judged by the same moral rules that constitute friendship. No true friend would do it or expect a friend to do it. In fact friendship is not the problem here but the solution. Suppose we ask how that insider dealing which is morally wrong – and only that which is – might be stopped. As the remarks from Tim Congdon quoted in an earlier chapter indicate, unethical acts in the tempestuous and fast moving flurry of financial markets may be very difficult to control by regulation. But one person at least should know when something wrong is being done and that is the person doing the unethical trading. Or rather he would know if he has an educated moral character and that character is sustained by the moral character and expectations, rewards and sanctions of those about him. Simon Green has remarked on the hubris in presuming that we each have within us, and with no help from others, the resources to successfully negotiate the moral world. Men are not perfect. They are subject to improving and degenerative forces. To be good they need all the help they can get. They need to talk about morally difficult decisions with friends. they need the approval and disapproval of friends to keep them on the straight and narrow. As Plato's dialogue form suggests, moral life involves dialogue.

Most of all they will be disciplined by the ultimate sanction of friendship which is ostracism, the end of the friendship. Those old boys' networks are crucially there to expel members who do not live up to standards; or indeed not to admit them in the first place. It was common for boys expelled from English schools such as

Harrow not to be asked to join the old boys' association; they were ex-Harrovians not Old Harrovians. Markets do indeed need moral institutions to work effectively and markets do not give rise to these institutions of law and morality. Nor do they sustain them. They are sustained by family, religion and friendship. There have always been two ways of stopping people in, say, a business, behaving badly. The first is to regulate and control all they do. The second is to regulate who comes in and stays in. And that second regulation is best done by informal social institutions. Formal procedures may be good at classifying what people do but informal associations are much better when it comes to who and what a person is.

And there may in reality be no choice between formal regulations and informal social sanctions. Even with a code, Lascelles points out:

> "[You] need to know who you are dealing with.
> You need to know more than is in the financial
> statement…in day to day trading or in a takeover
> you need to know the people involved…ultimately
> it's about trust and credibility".

It is of course as important to know who is untrustworthy as to know who is trustworthy. Both are essential in order to make something of the documents they produce. Even regulators need to know who is involved as well as what they appear to do.

Jamie Borwick gives another instance of the importance of friendship. He takes a practice generally disapproved of by the ethicists, that of two chief executives sitting as non-executive directors on each other's boards. The ethicists can easily spot the dangers of collusion and the non-executives giving the chief executive an excessively easy time in reward for getting an easy ride in their own capacity as chief executives. But if the two men are not conspirators but friends, the situation changes. Borwick argues that when it comes to giving a chief executive unwelcome advice and warnings, no-one has a better chance of being listened to than a friend. Against all the politically correct nostrums, the advice is taken not because it comes from a non-executive but a friend. From Aristotle to the letters to a current agony aunt, if there is one thing friendship is about it is giving and receiving frank advice.

And it is to the past one has to return to see this general point about friendship sustaining virtue, more particularly that about an individual's moral character needing the support and sanctions of friends. In modern political and business life the talk is of sleaze and corruption and the supposition is that friendship can lead to it. But listen to Shakespeare in Julius Caesar (Act I, Sc ii):

> *"Therefore it is meet*
> *That noble minds keep ever with their likes;*
> *For who so firm that cannot be seduced?"*[73]

and to Burke in his Letter to the Sheriffs of Bristol:

> *"The only method which has ever been found effectual*
> *to preserve any man against the corruption of nature*
> *and example, is an habit of life and communication of*
> *councils with the most virtuous and public-spirited men*
> *of the age you live in. Such a society cannot be kept*
> *without advantage or deserted without shame"*[74]

Here is the same Burke,

> *"I remember an old scholastic aphorism, which says,*
> *'that the man wholly detached from others, must be*
> *either an angel or a devil'. When I see in any of these*
> *detached gentlemen of our times the angelic purity,*
> *power, and beneficence, I shall admit them to be angels.*

---

[73] William Shakespeare, *Julius Caesar*, I, ii,
[74] Edmund Burke, "Letter to the Sheriffs of Bristol", in *On empire, liberty and reform*, (ed) David Bromwich, Yale University Press, 2000

> *In the mean time we are born only to be men. We shall*
> *do enough if we form ourselves to be good ones.*
> *It is therefore our business carefully to cultivate in our*
> *minds, to rear to the most perfect vigour and maturity,*
> *every sort of generous and honest feeling that belongs*
> *to our nature. To bring these dispositions that are*
> *lovely in private life into the service and conduct of the*
> *commonwealth; so to be patriots, as not to forget we*
> *are gentlemen. To cultivate friendships, and to incur*
> *enmities. To have both strong, but both selected:*
> *in the one, to be placable; in the other, immoveable".*[75]

If friendship can sustain high standards in business life, then to oust friendship from business life may actually lower standards. But it will do something else too. Friendship goes with the grain of human nature. Man enjoys friendship. Gary Shugg makes the point that laws and regulations which try to crush or eliminate "normal human responses" are silly and almost always wind up producing unintended and harmful consequences. For instance business people will willingly pay taxes – if they are not too high. To try to take too much of a person's reward for work or talent risks inciting dishonesty. So with regulations and friendship. Excessive regulation may turn virtuous friendships into vicious conspiracies.

CAN FRIENDSHIP STILL SUSTAIN UNIVERSITY LIFE?

A version of the doctrine of transparency plus some plain egalitarianism may also pose a threat to friendship in the university. As with business, the threat is not to friendship at universities. Students still make friends among themselves. Professors perhaps do not have as many friends among themselves with the decline of the single sex university and the decline of the university as a self-contained community. But the key is the part that friendship can and did play in scholarship.

---

[75] Edmund Burke, "Thoughts on the cause of the present discontents", in *Selected works of Edmund Burke vol I*, (ed) Francis Canavan, Liberty Fund, Indianapolis, 1999

Over the last two centuries many successful and justifiably famous men have passed through the universities. Re-reading their biographies, it is so often made clear that there they fell in with this or that individual or group, and that this friendship was significantly responsible for their education and success. Going up to a university used to mean much more than attending lectures, reading books, writing essays and passing exams. It used to mean joining a community and acquiring its values. That was why residency was so often a requirement for both students and, in some cases, staff – and why it still is so, if in a much more elastic way. Until the 1870s Oxford Colleges required residency within the college. But it also meant forming close ties with individuals and groups within the community.

Sometimes these involved students and staff. A student might learn to appreciate literature or discover a vocation for the church not only by book reading but by seeing love of literature or Christian ministry exhibited in the life of a tutor. The friendship that can grow up between tutor and taught when they find similar passions and convictions can provide the incentives for a further pursuit of knowledge and practice. Noel Annan[76] in his study *The Dons* notices that the charismatic John Henry Newman, while at Oxford "held himself responsible for his students' conduct. He was unique in treating them as his friends, and those who responded hung on his every word."

Many a student becomes a Christian or a Marxist, a lawyer or a biologist because of a person. That person may attract others to him and his ideas through his brilliance of thought or argument, through his courage, sincerity, kindness or some other quality. And he may not and does not need to become a friend for the attraction to happen. But in many cases friendship, of a sort, does ensue and plays its part.

---

[76] Noel Annan, *The Dons*, Harper Collins, London, 2000, p 40

135

Most of the literature on friendship argues that it is a relationship of equals. But here, this is not straightforwardly the case. A *mentor* is an experienced and trusted advisor. He knows more, has experienced more and is often older than his student-friend. Yet mentorship can be a friendship especially if in conversation the two parties behave as if they were equals. And if the relationship is long then the younger friend may increasingly draw nearer to the older in status and eventually go beyond him. Green suggests that a more careful look at the friendship classics shows that it is not so much equality that is necessary between friends but reciprocity. Both friends have to give something of worth though not necessarily at the same time and certainly not necessarily the same thing.

Friendships also exist between academic staff. And some of them are not just friendships of two or more academics but academic friendships. A well-known one was that small group called the *Inklings* just before, during and after the Second World War at Oxford. It consisted of C S Lewis, his brother, J R Tolkien and Charles Williams and some others. They met, read from the books they were writing and drank beer. In 1933 Tolkien wrote that his friendship with Lewis,

> *"besides giving constant pleasure and comfort, has*
> *done me much good from the contact with a man*
> *at once honest, brave, intellectual – a scholar, a poet,*
> *and a philosopher – and a lover, at least after a long*
> *pilgrimage, of Our Lord".*

This and what follows is from Humphrey Carpenter's *The Inklings*.[77]

Lewis himself describes the beginning of the friendship as based on a recognition that they were both fired by the same enthusiasm for "northern" myths. The friendship starts when someone who till then has believed his feelings to be unique cries out:

---

[77] Humphrey Carpenter, *The Inklings*, Unwin, London, 1981

"What? You too? I thought I was the only one".

This knowledge that someone sees the world as you do is, says Leo Strauss, central to intellectual endeavour and the pursuit of truth.

> *"The philosopher cannot lead an absolutely solitary*
> *life because legitimate 'subjective certainty' and the*
> *'subjective certainty' of the lunatic are indistinguishable.*
> *Genuine certainty must be 'inter-subjective'. The*
> *classics were fully aware of the essential weakness of*
> *the mind of the individual. Hence their teaching about*
> *the philosophic life is a teaching about friendship: the*
> *philosopher is, as a philosopher, in need of friends."*[78]

Aristotle stresses that friendships take time to grow. But that does not necessarily mean that they cannot start quite suddenly. Several of the academics interviewed for this book spoke about their own sudden friends. Professor James McCormick had a well-known intellectual partnership with Professor Petr Skrabanek. Together they wrote highly regarded books on the training of doctors. They were also great friends. But what is of interest in this context is that McCormick, a man given to weighing evidence and to a certain scepticism can say that,

> *"You know, with Petr, it was love at first sight...*
> *friendships can start like that with a glance and*
> *mutual recognition across a lecture hall"*.

The start of that friendship was like the immediate recognition of which Lewis speaks. Elaine Sternberg, another person known intellectually for not suffering nonsense, let alone sentimentality, admits to a twenty-second rule:

> *"I can usually tell in twenty seconds if I am going to be*
> *friends with someone."*

---

[78] Leo Strauss, *On tyranny, op cit* p194

The friendships make certain intellectual tasks easier too. Charles Williams spotted a special contribution of friendship to thought. Writing about the Inklings he said,

> *"Much was possible to a man in solitude, but some*
> *things were possible only to a man in companionship,*
> *and of these the most important was balance.*
> *No mind was so good that it did not need another*
> *to counter and equal it, and save it from conceit*
> *and bigotry and folly."*

Lewis, elsewhere, notes what friendship involves: a mutual delight in some idea or pastime, agreement not on answers but on questions, uninquisitiveness and absence of jealousy:

> *"You become a man's friend without knowing or caring*
> *whether he is married or single or how he earns his*
> *living…In each of my friends there is something that*
> *only another friend can bring out."*

And Lewis' brother Warnie shows just how deep the friendship was when he recalls in his diary Charles Williams' sudden death:

> *"One often reads of people being 'stunned' by bad*
> *news…there is more than a little truth in it. I felt just*
> *as if I had slipped and come down on my head on the*
> *pavement…I felt dazed and restless, and went to get a*
> *drink: choosing unfortunately the King's Arms, where*
> *during the winter Charles and I more than once drank*
> *a pint after leaving Tollers at the Mitre…There will be*
> *no more pints with Charles: the blackout has fallen,*
> *and the Inklings can never be the same again."*

Most important in these remarks are those ones which link friendship to scholarship, those about honesty, mutual passion for a subject, balance and the absence of "jealousy, bigotry and folly."

Such friendships are not always popular outside the circle of friends. McCormick cheerfully admits that his special friendship with Skrabanek, a member of the department he led, gave rise to "considerable jealousy". But a more topical question is whether there are not developments in today's universities which threaten friendship and the scholarly results it produces. Simon Green identified three general developments. Academic friendships have declined because of a decline in communal life – societies, dining clubs etc; because of a decline in common interests as academics cease to be educated men and become academic specialists; and because of a decline in common values as the academic ethos is replaced by competitive careerism and bureaucracy. Green also draws attention to the change that has taken place in academic collaboration in the humanities and social sciences. It used to be between friends. Now most young economists, for instance, collaborate serially with different people at different times and for different instrumental purposes.

There is room, of course, for friendship in the modern university but not mixed with work. The trouble with this is that for Lewis and his friends, friendship was essential to their scholarship – it is quite possible that *The Lord of the Rings* would not have been completed without the support of the friends. Friendship too can sustain the work of the intellect outside the university. The correspondence between authors such as Evelyn Waugh and Nancy Mitford or, in the United States between Walker Percy and Shelby Foote is sometimes referred to as "literary friendship" as if it were, in some way unlike normal friendship, a special category or sub-category of it. And of course in both these and many other cases such as that of Philip Larkin and Kingsley Amis the friendship was indeed literary in two senses, that it was carried on largely by written words in letters and that many of those letters were about the correspondents' shared craft. Foote, says the man who edited the Percy-Foote correspondence, Jay Tolson, "was [Percy's] brother in art, his secret sharer".[79] In a letter of 1979 Percy wrote to Foote,

> *"You, for example, know exactly what I am talking about because you are a writer and because we have known each other forever – and because we are Southern."*[80]

But this does not mean that, like all good friendships, it did not involve virtues: for instance those of honesty and trust, the ability to confide and chide and take chiding, mutual moral dispositions and humour, any more than it lacked the characteristics of non-literary friendships such as sheer pleasure at being together. Elsewhere Foote wrote:

> *"I'd like to come down with Gwyn for a three or four week stay in the guest house, doing the final typescript. We'd do our own cooking and everything… We could work all day and talk all night. I think it's a great shame we've been apart so much these past three-four years. Friendship is so rare a thing, it should never be neglected beyond necessity."*[81]

FRIENDSHIP IN MEDICINE, THE CHURCH AND THE ARMY

One profession where friendship still appears to thrive is medicine. Dr James Le Fanu discerns various levels and types of friendship. Doctors take a strong part in community and voluntary organizations. Many are active members of churches, many are Rotarians and a substantial number are Freemasons, especially doctors from teaching hospitals. In these organizations they make friends with people from all sorts of occupations. But they may also have friendships with members of their profession. It is difficult to know, however, whether these should be classified as professional friendships. In some cases two doctors may choose to work together for instance

---

[79] *The correspondence of Shelby Foote and Walker Percy* edited by Jay Tolson, Norton, New York, 1998, p 1
[80] *Ibid* p 2
[81] *Ibid* Letter 6 October, 1956

a surgeon and an anaesthetist. The friendship might come out of working together but then the friendship might encourage them to try to work together when possible. And doctors make friends with other doctors, at least they did so, in training. These friends they often keep. And past similarities can even encourage friendships many years later. A doctor can meet another who is a complete stranger and within seconds they can establish common experiences: "you trained at St X's in the seventies, you must have known Y, been taught by Z, I suppose if you are now in A you must have come across B". This common background was not any background. According to Le Fanu, the London medical schools of the seventies were not only very highly regarded but a sort of club. Their members felt part of a historical tradition. And it was a club which had, as it were, reciprocal arrangements all over the world. He cites one famous liver specialist, Dame Sheila Sherlock, who could survey the globe and find thirty-five professors whom she'd taught or worked with, who "were all her friends". There was something else that bound doctors together at that time too. It was a time of great advance in medicine and "the revolution in medicine bound people together as co-pioneers".

The comparative decline of London's schools and what Le Fanu sees as the end of the revolution, together with the massive bureaucratisation of the NHS and medical training may have hit friendship too. But there are still institutional aspects of medicine that support friendship. After training, reading the same journals provides common ground and the conference circuit provides opportunities for old friendships to be unfrozen and up-dated. There is still something special, he thinks, about medical friendships. Doctors, he suggests, tend to have several doctors among their friends though, especially in general practice, not those they work with. The tie seems to be that doctoring is a serious business. It involves knowledge of pain, distress, embarrassment and the common knowledge of these binds doctors together. This seems to me a very clear instance of the Aristotelian friendship, one founded on a common moral purpose.

But there is one other sort of friendship which takes us back to friendship in universities. Medicine, in the United Kingdom, has thrown up some famous and long-lasting research friendships – Le Fanu mentions those of Sir Richard Doll and Austin Bradford Hill, later of Doll and Sir Richard Peto, of Patrick Steptoe and Bob Edwards, of George Hitchings and Gertrude Elion. These are interesting for two reasons. They may start as a more famous and senior man with a younger, junior and even unknown one, but this difference, this inequality does not make friendship impossible. As years pass, the "pupil" status gets nearer that of the "master". Second, though the two are no doubt united by a common exposure to "serious" matters, their special common experience is to be co-innovators or co-creators.

If this analysis is correct we can readily identify what the enemies of friendship in medicine might be. They have been encountered before in this book especially in the section on business. Medical friendships depend on close experiences, many of which are personal. Anything which removes personal discretion, which anonymises relations between doctors or between doctors and patients, which scientizes medicine at the expense of its humaneness will spell trouble not just for medicine but for friendships too.

THE CHURCH

The friendships of several famous priests are well known. And what is noteworthy is that the friends of Augustine or Newman, for instance, were often other priests. Priests certainly might be expected to have a shared moral outlook. And yet one very senior Anglican cleric, John Simpson, at one time a Director of Ordinands, an archdeacon – and thus overseeing the clergy of a diocese – and the dean of his communion's principal cathedral, Canterbury, suggests that the clergy today are not generally noted for deep friendships with each other. The clergy of a town or district of a city rarely make deep friends with each other. Most of the friendships they do have with other clergy date from the time of their training, especially those whom they trained with. Some go beyond it; what makes a man understand that he has a vocation for the priesthood is often not so much a direct intellectual conviction as the example of an older priest whom he admires and who is, or becomes his friend. Clever church administrators who wish to increase vocations in their area know that having several of these holy and friendly priests in their diocese will do more than any plan. The number of Anglican clergy is falling. That means there are some who have not attracted a single "replacement". In fact quite probably a lot, because, says Simpson, he knows others who may have attracted dozens. And more to the point here, they keep them as friends.

Shared moral purpose seems not to be enough. Simpson even has doubts as to whether cells – that is, prayer groups of clergy – result in many friendships. Friendship is crucially voluntary. Friends are attracted to their friends, in McCormick's words cited earlier, by "love at first sight" or, in Montaigne's, because you are you and I am I. It's this attraction plus the shared moral purpose which grounds friendship and the two together, in the case of clergy as in the case of medical researchers, can easily overcome differences in age, fame and status.

What could threaten these friendships? Obviously anything which destroyed the community aspects of the theological college or made unlikely the continued existence, employment and influence of those holy and attractive priests. In an increasingly bureaucratic church which wants figures achieved and procedures followed, their quiet influence may go unnoticed.

THE ARMY

"As a cadet at Sandhurst, a training college for British army officers, one was initially thrown together with a host of people whom one had not met before. You soon realised that you could be posted to the same unit with a small number of your contemporaries from Sandhurst. You also realized that whether you liked them or not, you could be with these people for many years to come. One had no choice but at least to try to get on with them. In fact, this common experience often produced long-lasting friendships. The nature of being in an Army unit is that your working colleagues and your chums are often one and the same.

If you can imagine being transported, aged 20, from Sandhurst to some remote part of the globe such as Malaya, to an isolated garrison, you could find yourself joining, say, a group of 20 other officers of varying ages. You were in fact really joining a family. If, unfortunately, you found it difficult to get on with the others in this small community, then probably you would move on to somewhere else. Most of the friends at least initially were within one's age group and of a similar rank. But the longer one was there, the wider the extent of one's friendships could grow. It was essential that you had positive relationships with your fellow officers, both on and off duty. This situation contrasted with the one which can be found when one left the services and joined a commercial company. In this instance, most people had two lives which did not cross over much. One was their working life, and the other their private, and there were very few people who had friends at work whom they also considered friends in the home environment.

Another aspect of service life is that probably the most important element that everyone wishes to preserve is the status of the unit or 'the regiment'. Everyone, from the highest to the lowest in the organization, invariably wants to do their best for the 'regiment'. The regiment wants to be seen in the main in a good light. If, for instance, particular relationships are not helping the cohesion of the unit, then obviously something has to be done about it. This can be seen at a higher level in that if a unit is on active service, the strength of the friendships could be critically important if one's friends-colleagues are to survive in dangerous circumstances.

It is possible to say that within a service environment, almost in the terms of an 'arranged marriage', friendships are made and some of them can be very, very strong friendships that last for life. Even in a strongly hierarchical institution such as the Army, common dangers and common moral outlooks can produce friendships and loyalties which transcend the rank structure."

Much of the conventional wisdom on friendship blithely says it is a voluntary affair between equals. In this interview, a British army colonel, who, after retirement from the service, worked in business, shows that both the assumption about voluntariness and equality can be challenged, at least as far as the Army is concerned. We might ask what could threaten these army friendships. Anything which broke up the continuity of association such as the erosion of regiments, the regarding of soldiers as individual moveable employees, short term contracts, the decline of a martial culture. But one other: in the interview, the officer mentioned that the demands of the regiment, that is the army and the friends, could come into conflict with the demands of officers' and men's wives. In his day, "the regiment came first; now, it wouldn't happen." It is time to consider the complex relationship of friends and families.

It is not just ideologies of equality and transparency or bureaucratizing tendencies which can undermine friendship. Friendship is also in tension with other loyalties in the more personal sphere, especially those to romantic love and marriage. As the modern family has become increasingly nuclear, one obligation has taken precedence over others. Husband and wife still have important obligations to their own and each other's middle-aged parents, residual and largely token obligations to cousins and aunts, ill-defined and, I suspect ill-protected obligations to their brothers and sisters, but the central obligation is to each other and their children.

How much room does this leave for friends?

Overleaf

Detail *Promis'd Horrors of the French Invasion* James Gillray

CHAPTER SEVEN

FRIENDSHIP'S GREEDY RIVAL FOR TIME AND AFFECTION: THE ROMANTIC FAMILY

"[Sexual] love from its very nature must be transitory. To seek for a secret that would render it constant would be a wild search for the philosopher's stone or the grand panacea: and the discovery would be equally useless, or rather, pernicious to mankind. *The most holy bond of society is friendship.*"[82]

ROMANTIC MARRIAGE AND THE INCREASED DEMAND ON SPOUSES

The move from extended to nuclear family has been accompanied by an emphasis on the romantic and sexual love between husband and wife. A great deal is expected of that relationship. For instance, a wedding, once seen as an alliance between two families and possibly properties, and arranged and supervised by the bride's parents is now seen as the culmination of a personal relationship to which the couple invite others, if they choose. Husbands and wives are expected to do more together, to take more joint decisions, to remain in a state of romantic love for many years. The huge,

---

[82] Mary Wollstonecraft, *A vindication of the rights of women*, London, 1972

and some would say unrealistic expectations of marriage or "partnership", in part explain the large number of unions which break up. Some couples divorce because they do not feel romantic love for each other, and society, at least some of it, agrees that this is a suitable reason for divorce.

ROMANTIC IDEALS OF CHILDREN AND THE INCREASED DEMANDS ON PARENTS

If the modern ideal of marriage is romantic so is the ideal of children. Parents are expected not only to love children but to feel as if they love them, to demonstrate their affection for them, to be with them. If a mother or father does not spend adequate time with children, this is commented on and "adequate" means a lot. In keeping with this, other people, grandparents, neighbours and friends are expected to approach children, as it were, through parents and with their permission.

Thus the nuclear family is very turned in on itself both in terms of time, activities and emotions. This is a fairly new state of affairs. One illustrative example: as late as the nineteen fifties many middle-class but not very affluent families made severe financial sacrifices to send their children to fee-paying independent schools. Many were boarding schools and that cost additional financial effort. One set of parents who made such efforts were those of only-children. And these children were dispatched to the boarding schools as early as seven or eight years old. Today there is still an independent sector but far less boarding, very little boarding at such an early age, and during the boarding there are now frequent parental visits or weekends at home. In the fifties it was not uncommon for schools to have a rule of no parental contact during the first 14-week term and thereafter only every three weeks for half a Sunday.

Cynics suggested that the parents were "getting rid" of their children so they could continue to enjoy themselves unhampered by the responsibilities of childcare. In fact many of these parents made not only a financial sacrifice but an emotional one. Many of the mothers especially were as upset when their children went away as were their children. And that was the reason they did it. The parents, especially those with only children, were concerned lest their children become too wrapped up in their small families. They wanted them to make friends, to learn to get on with adults other than parents. They were prepared to be unhappy without their children – and for their children to be unhappy – to prevent these children growing up in just the romantic tightly-knit tiny unit that is now seen as ideal.

If the modern family is undergirded by romantic, sometimes sentimental, assumptions in relations both between husband and wife and between them and their children, it is also undergirded with assumptions about friends. A husband is expected to love, feel for, desire his wife and show it; he is also expected to be her companion and friend, and she his. Parents are expected to dote on their children but also be their "friends", someone they can talk to as equals. The combination of romantic, tightly knit and friendly expectations is a tall order and , some might argue, a very confused and contradictory one. But that is not our concern. What are the implications for friendship?

FRIENDSHIP AS AN INGREDIENT OF MODERN MARRIAGE

In one sense the new family provides a new opportunity for friendship, a new ground on which it can operate. Who can doubt that in many successful marriages, and that usually means long-lived marriages, it is mutual companionship, friendship that sustains the marriage? *The Book of Common Prayer* gives the third purpose of marriage as "the mutual society, help and comfort that the one ought to have of the other both in prosperity and adversity".

The (old) Roman *Small Ritual* speaks of husband and wife being "united in love for Thee".

This language of shared moral purpose, mutual support, two becoming one, this mention of hardship and mutual pleasure and comfort is a language common to friendship and marriage. Just how big a role friendship played in marriages in past times is disputed with variations between classes and places: Montaigne, for instance, is quite clear that your wife is not your friend; you find friendship elsewhere. Perhaps this is a peculiarly French or Latin view. What is clear is that today in modern societies, there is a family which is very small, democratic, ideally almost a family of equals, very busy emotionally and in activities, within itself, very long-lasting, dominated by ideals of romanticism and friendship. Thus friendship has a new or added lease of life.

On the other hand, this new family demands a lot of allegiance. It is jealous of its members having affections or activities outside of itself with friends. In Simon Green's words,

> *"Romantic marriage drives out friendship. It is not only exclusive, it is greedy. It goes on and on eating up other areas of life…All friends are potentially suspect because they are potential rivals to the highest form [of friendship, i.e. the family]…And romantic notions of children also displace social forms, again the biological excluding the social…or the willed."*

Thus this nexus of activities and expectations around the biological unit, the family, is in tension and rivalry with activities and affections of social and voluntary forms of association.

> *"Friendship is being oozed out of life…and there is a profound irony here…the irony is that the modern family does not work. It's not just divorce. We marry*

*late so we have ten more years of life outside the
family...we get divorced and have more years of life
outside the family...and as the rights of individuals are
more and more stressed there will be more and more
children we don't like; that is, where liking or not
becomes a voluntary act."*

Let us see if we can clarify this: What is being argued is that modern
ideals of life centre on the family and that other forms such as
friendship are squeezed out. Elsewhere Green argues that the
universalistic ideals of modern justice also squeeze out particular
affections in friendship. It is that we are allowed as it were two
domains of life, one governed by universal ideals, one by particular.
The two do not get on, but both squeeze out friendship, the
particular because it is dominated by one acceptable form, family
life, the universal because it condemns particular affections as
"tribal". This does not mean we actually spend more time in the
family which for a variety of reasons is failing. But it does mean
there is no acceptance, no ideal, no code of friendship to govern
those friendships which arise in between successive family obligations or when families fail.

*"So we want friendships, we keep trying to make them,
but they fail because we are no good at them, because
we have been dominated by an ideal of family affection
and activity. We certainly make what we call friendships
but because we don't know how to do so properly
and have little guidance through sophisticated social
expectations, what we actually get are bogus
friendships...as in sitcoms...we've lost it, our lives are
thin and self-consciously unfulfilled, we know there's
something wrong but we can't put it back."*

In Ray Pahl's *On friendship*[83] he, like Green, notes the crumbling of

---

[83] Ray Pahl, *On friendship, op cit*

153

the old family. But he welcomes the opportunity for new and diverse forms of association including friendship. Where he and Green differ is that Green thinks the new opportunities for friendship are unlikely to be fulfilled because we no longer have, as a society, a sophisticated idea of how to make and keep friends, what to give to and expect from them. And the modern family is partially responsible for this collapse, not in our desire for friendships but in our knowledge and practice of them.

Whether one accepts this or not, it would be a blind person who did not see that families can come into rivalry with and conflict with friendships. The potential for tension has been noted some time ago. Samuel Butler wrote in the nineteenth century:

> *"A man's friendships, are, like his will, invalidated by marriage – but they are no less invalidated by the marriage of his friends. The rift in friendship which invariably makes its presence on the marriage of either of the parties to it was fast widening [with the marriage of Ernest Pontifex to Ellen], as it no less invariably does, into the great gulf which is fixed between the married and the unmarried."* [84]

Charles Lamb is even more caustic. He warns any friend of a groom,

> *"If the husband with whom you have lived on a friendly footing before marriage, – if you did not come in on the wife's side, – if you did not sneak into the house in her train, but were an old friend in fast habits of intimacy before their courtship was as much as thought of, – look about you – your tenure is precarious – before a twelvemonth shall roll over your head, you shall find your old friend gradually grow cool and altered towards you, and at last seek opportunities of breaking with you".* [85]

---

[84] Samuel Butler, *The way of all flesh*, Bestseller Library, Paul Elek Ltd, London, 1958, p 315
[85] Charles Lamb, "A bachelor's complaint" in *The complete works of Charles Lamb*, Chatto and Windus, London, 1892

Since he wrote, modern marriage has an increased variety of ways of damaging friendships. It may simply be that some former friends are unacceptable to a spouse. It may be that, for instance, the husband is allowed a specific time or activity with a friend or group of friends, Saturday at the football match or golf course. Certainly any sort of alternative home, most notably the single sex gentleman's club, is frowned on. Indeed it may soon be illegal. Green acutely notices that

> *"the real reason for single sex clubs was not to nurture*
> *single sex relationships but to exclude the family...to*
> *provide an area of life where the family may not enter"*.

We have already seen how friendship is being driven from the high ground of society, most of all from the work place. If the family restricts its licence in recreation, then there will be few places left where friendship is the predominant mode of association. Even the pub is increasingly being colonized by couples who talk to each other, but not to other couples.

The romantic marriage has further trouble in store for friends. When it fails, as so often it does, divorce plays havoc with friendship, with friends, and more importantly leads to their own spouses being forced to agree to take sides in the conflict and subsequent separated lives. When re-marriage occurs, it involves changes in the character and interests of the new couple that may effectively exclude friends. This is particularly the case when the man marries a new and much younger wife.

Friendship then is often called upon to fight its corner. A husband or wife will have to justify time spent with friends instead of the wife or husband. When he tries to do this he will find little ammunition because of the unacknowledged role of friendship is society. Grandparents can advance the claims of grandparenthood, even siblings the claims of brother or sister, but there just does not exist a set of claims or obligations of friendship on which society is agreed.

CASE STUDIES OF MARRIAGE AND FRIENDSHIP

Consider some of the ways that marriage can erode friendship. First, two cases about couples, movement and friendship.

CASE 1: THE NEWLY-WEDS PURSUING CAREERS

George and Jean got married shortly after both had graduated from university. Both had friends from their schooldays and home days with whom they had kept in touch while at university. They had seen their school and home friends during visits especially during university vacations. Both also made several friends at university.

After marriage, both of them looked for jobs. Their aim was to find the jobs that paid the most and offered good career prospects. This was awkward because they also wanted two jobs fairly close to each other. The couple shared the common view that married persons should not be separated for long by physical distance. Eventually they went to live in a city several hours travel from their parents' homes and the university city. Further changes of job and moves up the career ladder brought further changes of address. After six or seven years they had lost contact with nearly all their university friends and with all but three of their home friends.

At first sight this seems to be not a case of the effects of marriage on friendship but of moving home on friendship. It is a commonplace that modern society is characterized by frequent job changes, frequent changes of address and increased distance between various addresses. Such mobility is said to make the maintenance of friendship difficult.

Indeed it does. However it only makes it difficult not impossible. Modern society is also characterized by rapid transport and longer work vacations, by telephone, fax and e-mail – and affluence which pays for contact and travel. All help in keeping in touch. Of course contact can be lost for a time. But friendship has a peculiar attribute in that frozen friendships, when contact is re-established, seem to take off where they left off. Friendship can take long periods of separation.

It is interesting that I have, without thinking, used the phrase "lost contact" as if it were some sort of accident. Perhaps "neglect" might be a more suitable term. "Neglect" has more than a touch of disapproval about it. If someone did not keep in contact with his parents, his bank account, if he did not feed the dog for two or three days he would not be allowed to get away with pleading that he had lost contact or that it was some sort of accident. "Neglect" unlike "lost contact" implies an obligation and one recognized by society, the breach of which results in social disapproval. Dr Johnson's advice was that friendships should be kept in constant repair. George and Jean have been neglectful. Or perhaps they did not really value their friendship, for when we lose something we value, we quickly miss it and search long and hard for it until we find it. Modern society has little to say about George and Jean's loss or about whether it constitutes neglect. It also has little to say about whether friends, unlike married persons, should keep in physical proximity. Modern society has little to say about the desirability or otherwise of keeping friendships in repair. Modern society issues no such advice and none of the reprobation implicit in it.

George and Jean have neglected their friends and neglected friendship. Why? There could be a number of reasons, which, were the neglect one of any other relationship than friendship, might be called laziness, ingratitude and selfishness. Or it might be that the two of them are so caught up in their new marriage and jobs, in the frantic busyness of their new life, that old friends get forgotten.

What is of interest is that this busyness would certainly pass as an acceptable reason for their "neglect" of friends if offered as such to most modern persons including, maybe the friends themselves. Here what undermines friendship is a combination of the high view of the husband-wife relationship and the importance of getting the right job and house and the very low view of friendship and its obligations.

Perhaps we should not feel too sorry for the neglected friends, since most of them will be busy with their spouses, jobs and houses and neglecting their friends, including George and Jean. Have such friendships ended? Not in all cases. It is not unknown when George, Jean or both have some crisis of money or health for them to go back over the years to old neglected friends in the search for help. Nor is it unknown for their friends to give it.

CASE 2: CHOOSING A PLACE TO RETIRE TO

Bill and Eileen are 65 and 63 years old respectively. They have lived in their current home in a medium sized town for twenty something years and been planning their retirement. And they have chosen to move to a part of the country which they "discovered" about six years ago and where since, they have had several happy holidays. They have chosen it partly because they have enjoyed themselves there and partly because house prices are much cheaper and the move will unlock a third of the price of their current house to help them pay for the retirement. Bill's parents are dead and Eileen's mother lives nearer the retirement house than their current address. Their only other close family, their daughter, Gina, lives in Canada.

Eileen has been on a retirement course. The lecturer there urged her class to remember the matter of friends. She explained how older people may need friends. Eileen takes the point. She has noted how friendly the people are where they are thinking of retiring and has no doubt she and Bill will make friends easily. As with George and

Jean's thinking, friends seem to be viewed as rather less than domestic animals. And again as with George and Jean, what is crucial is not what marriage does directly to friendship but what society's view of friendship and marriage in the priority of obligations seems to be.

The retirement course literature and social chatter both agree that retirement needs planning. The most important thing is that the couple should talk about what they want together; that they should consider their health, their finances, their mobility etc. Somewhere on this list, rather low down are friends. But the concept of friendship involved is a very restricted one. These "friends" are more a mutual aid insurance bet than any genuine friendship.

Both Eileen and the lecturer understand the matter of friendship to consist largely in what friends can do for Eileen. No mention has been made of what she can do for them or aspects of friendship which have little to do with functions. Little thought has been given to the obligations Bill and she owe to the friends they have where they are. She also appears to think that friends can be discarded and new ones acquired – replacements – fairly easily. Of course some friendships are formed very quickly but it is an odd view of friendship which assumes this is there for the asking and can be relied upon to happen. Eileen has no friends where she is going yet. She is assuming that because the people are generally "friendly", i.e. polite and welcoming, that this means several of them will become her friends.

Being friendly has little to do with being friends. And it is a very low view of friendship which can mistake the one for the other. How bizarre her view of friendship is can be seen if it is contrasted with her view of marriage and her husband. She does not assume that he should be casually discarded or would be easily replaceable.

There are other cases which can be dealt with more quickly because they are simpler to describe

CASE 3: BABIES VERSUS FRIENDS

Edward and Sue have recently been married. Eddie has two long-standing (male) friends one of whom he goes fishing with, one of whom he meets for a drink several nights a week after work. He also has other friends he sees less often. Sue wants the fishing trip and the pub visits to stop. She says he ought to spend time with her now that he is married. Sometimes she says that the money spent on fishing and drinks is their money, not his, and should be spent on the house. Sometimes she suggests they ought to go out together. When they do, and when he persuades her they should go out together to the pub, she is polite enough to Edward's friend but no-one enjoys him or herself very much. Sometimes Edward feels that she would like to go out but elsewhere. She is socially ambitious and thinks the pub friend is the wrong sort of friend. As for the fishing trip, she thinks it simply takes up too much time, sometimes all Saturday; what is she supposed to do all day?

This seems to be a fairly common story of marriage-friendship conflict especially when the couple are both young. If the conflict is not a problem immediately after marriage, it becomes one later when Sue has her children. Then the competition for Edward's time, money, presence and affection is not only between Sue and the friends but Sue and the baby/children and his friends.

Some couples who marry later or where there is an age difference or who are more affluent or where there is support from a wider family may have less of a problem. Sometimes the Edwards and Sues ration out opportunities and moneys for friendship successfully; you go out on Tuesdays with your friends; I'll see mine on Thursdays. Sometimes tensions are made worse by jealousy. Here it is not the time spent away or the money spent but the "rival" affection that is a problem.

Such emotional matters are made worse by the lack of social rules. If Green is right then society increasingly favours the case of the family against that of the friends. But perhaps more grave is the lack of established habits and institutions that either side can appeal too. It is this which makes the dispute personal. The Victorian solution was that society recognized the rights of, in particular married men, to spend time with friends in clubs, pubs and at sports. To a lesser extent there were clubs and activities for ladies too. Modern standards would find this an unfair solution to the problem because it favoured the man's preferences. But at least there was a solution at societal level. And at least the wife could complain about what "men" did rather than feel it as a personal neglect.

CASE 4: DIVORCE AND FRIENDS

Richard and Jane have got over the sorts of problems that Edward and Sue had. They have, as a couple, four couples who are their friends, friends, that is, to both of them. The problem is that, like over a third of other married couples, they are getting divorced and like many of those others, theirs is an acrimonious divorce. Their friends have to choose which one of them to remain friends with.

Divorce, probably, has an enormous impact on friendship and it is mostly destructive. Often it can halve the number of friendships which continue. Or even more because at least one divorced spouse also moves away and that means moving away from friends as well as spouse. In balance it has to be said that divorced individuals often seek comfort, advice and time with their friends and that can revive old friendships at least for a while.

CASE 5: REMARRIAGE AND FRIENDS

Richard is aged 55 and divorced from Jane. He has a number of friends including several to whom he has become even closer since his divorce. Many of them share his enthusiasms for watching rugby and eating and drinking. He has now married for a second time.

His new wife, Kim, is aged 36. She is keen to re-brand him and not only calls him Dicky but explains to his friends that Dicky is now what he is called. She jogs and goes to the gym and so now does he. Of course, he can see his friends but he can't do so at pubs and restaurants. He is not the Richard his friends knew. Gradually he sees less of them. Indeed she has new younger friends she wants him to meet.

The ancients saw "permanence of character" as the key to friendship. I am friends with you because of your character and remain so because you are the same person you were. Richard or "Dicky" is not the same character. He has reinvented himself to please Kim.

MARRIAGE AND FRIENDSHIP: A REAL CONFLICT

It will not come as a surprise to any friend or married person to see these real tensions between the family and friendship. They are well-known in everyday life. But, curiously, they are far from well-known in social philosophy and political theory. During the last twenty years there has been a resurgence of intellectual interest in the non-state institutions of society, in "community" and "civil society" and intermediate institutions between the individual and the state. A good society needs not just good central government and free markets, not even just these and the rule of law, but a morality, manners and habits, sociability and harmony, taught and maintained through institutions such as the family, neighbourhoods, churches, voluntary groups and leisure associations.

Two things are interesting about this new thinking. The first is that friendship is seldom mentioned though it is surely one of these institutions. The second is that it is usually assumed that while these institutions might sometimes be in conflict with the state, they are essentially in harmony with each other. In the case of friendship, this is simply not true. And I doubt whether it is true of the others either.

Diana
Princess of Wales · Queen of H

CHAPTER EIGHT

THE DECLINE OF FRIENDSHIP:
THE LOSS OF VIRTUE AND MANNERS

VIRTUE AND FRIENDSHIP

If this book is right, people today are losing their friends. They may have the same number of friends but the friends they have now are not as good friends as the friends their parents had. Why has this happened? One way to answer this might be to look at other things we have lost in this modern age and see if they are tied up with the loss of friends.

Elsewhere I have argued that there has been a more general decline in morals and manners. Let's take the moral decline. What has been seen in the last half century has been a "loss of virtue".[86] Since the classical understanding of friendship makes it either a virtue itself or dependent on the virtues such as loyalty and trust, a loss of friendship might well be associated with any decline in virtue. There are further ties. This book has identified three ways in which one might assert a decline in friendship: first a decline in the practice of friendship with it becoming shallower, restricted from public life and

---

[86] Digby Anderson (ed), *The loss of virtue: moral confusion and social disorder in Britain and America*, Social Affairs Unit, London, 1992

165

largely recreational; second, a decline in the public acknowledgment of friendship's role; and third and last, a growing inability to think and talk in a sophisticated and coherent way about friendship.

Similarly, one might assert a loss of virtue in at least three senses. Our behaviour might be less virtuous; for instance there might be more sexual promiscuity and less courage. Second the role of virtue in the maintenance of social order (once highly valued by those on the political right) and social justice (similarly valued by those on the left) might be less acknowledged than in previous societies. Instead other "causes" of social disorder and injustice might be substituted such as social structural factors – unemployment or low income, loss of self-esteem or political factors – estrangement from political government. Third, loss of virtue might be understood as a loss of articulateness about moral matters.

To illustrate the first: Christie Davies has pointed both to the surge of crime, self-destructive behaviour and social disorder in the last seventy-odd years and to the reduction in crime in Britain, in the nineteenth and early twentieth century.[87] The experience of the last 150 years is a U curve. The Victorians inherited what they considered high rates of crime and illegitimacy (8%) and more than halved them. The explanation for the subsequent rise in crime and illegitimacy cannot be convincingly sought in structural factors such as poverty or poor housing since both were worse in the low crime and disorder period than they were in the high crime and disorder period. The explanation, according to Davies, lies in a change of national moral character, an increase in the number of aggressive, self-destructive people, the reduction of conscience and self-control, and the provision of moral excuses. This anti-moral movement has been promoted by progressive intellectuals.

For the second case, that virtue has declined in that its role is no longer acknowledged in the maintenance of order and justice,

---

[87] *Ibid* Ch 1

I merely refer to the corpus of sociology and social policy textbooks of the last half century. For a particular instance, consider the contemporary analysis of poverty. I have argued elsewhere that domestic poverty is not simply the result of low incomes but is affected by competence in saving and expenditure, by family budgeting and the management of debt.[88] Often it is poor domestic economy or imprudence that turns temporary low income into long-term poverty. Low income families which get out of poverty do so through a range of characterological virtues including meticulous stewardship, self-denial, and especially in the wife's case, self-sacrifice. In all the poverty literature I have encountered this virtue aspect is conspicuously and, I think, deliberately avoided.

This refusal to acknowledge the role of virtue is bound up with the third loss which also needs more specific illustration, the loss of articulateness about the virtues. Simon Green has argued that the two important quasi-virtues of manliness and civility are both misunderstood today.[89] The first is seen as male aggression, the second is seen as insufficiently virtuous, a mere formal accommodation of other fellow citizens. In fact the two go together. Manliness makes civility possible. Manliness is not maleness; women can be manly. It is the opposite of animality. It is the control of the innate, the modest cultivation and improvement of the common sum of man's attributes, the best of what is human. It is not heroic or saintly, still less priestly. Nor is civility which does not sacrifice to others but quietly recognizes their rights and the importance of each going his own way. It is the bourgeois virtue of privacy and limited publicness. Both manliness and civility rely on a self-control and ordinariness which are distinctly unfashionable.

John Gray has argued that modern society misunderstands toleration as moral neutrality.[90] True toleration is unfashionable because it assumes human imperfectability and because it assumes evils to be

---

[88] *Ibid* Ch 4
[89] *Ibid* Ch 2
[90] *Ibid* Ch 3

tolerated and thus is inherently judgmental. It also offends against equality and implicitly elevates a basic culture embodying the virtue of toleration itself. Neutrality wants to abolish prejudice and incorrect thinking, that is, non-neutral thinking. Toleration leaves people alone and in peace. Toleration is at odds with the therapeutic ideal in its acceptance of imperfection and its judgementalism.

We might continue our tour of old ideas by inspecting the way honour, honesty and trust helped society to police itself, how diligence was central to the understanding of education and schooling, how respect protected valuable institutions from unrestrained criticism, how discretion made fine distinctions between, for instance, the deserving and undeserving. But enough has been said to show the argument. It is that there was once a sophisticated and elaborate list of virtues, perhaps some twenty of them, certainly not the care and compassion that monopolise the field today. These twenty virtues were applied by an equally fine casuistry. Both the list and the science of its application to social problems is not understood today. Insofar as the virtues were morality, we may talk of modern society being morally illiterate, a loss of virtue in deed and in thought and culture.

PARTICULAR VIRTUES AND FRIENDSHIP

If such a decline in general virtue is generally ominous for friendship as a virtuous institution, then the decline of particular virtues on which classical friendship relies is even more so. These are fidelity, trust, honour, candour and truthfulness and self-sacrifice. Patricia Morgan has shown how fidelity has become a casualty of the new contractual understanding of marriage.[91] Obviously fidelity has come into conflict with the contemporary emphasis on self-fulfiment. But even when it is admitted, it tends to be thought of in a strictly legalistic, contractarian way. In marital break-up for instance if fault in admitted at all it is legalistic fault, a default of contract. Whereas

---

[91] *Ibid* Ch 7

what used to be pointed to was infidelity. The obligation of fidelity is unconditional. It comes with the status of being a husband or wife and is not reduced by the other's faults. It is not re-negotiable. A wife's infidelity did not mean that a husband was freed from his obligation to be faithful.

A marriage in which each party continues to love, help, be with, do things for, give up one's own desires for the other on the condition that the other does the same is no true marriage in the traditional sense and it shows no true love, self-sacrifice or fidelity. What it is, is a *contract*, a deal. Although friendship can come into rivalry with marriage in the competition for someone's time and affections, we have already seen that friendship shares many characteristics with marriage (perhaps that is why they are in competition). The ideal friendship like marriage is mutual and reciprocal but it is not entered into for the gains of mutuality or reciprocity.

It is based on fidelity not contract. It is true that the demands of fidelity in friendship are different from those of marriage, at least some ideas of marriage. There is no necessary dishonour, if friends find that their friendship is over, whereas some marriages are "till death us do part". But a society in which the virtue of fidelity is replaced by the mutual self-interest of contract is not a society which will be kind to friendship. And a society which has ceased to understand fidelity will not understand true friendship or that the obligations of friendship bear strong similarities to those of marriage. If the marriage virtues are undermined – and contemporary divorce rates and the way contemporary society talks about marriage as a contract, suggest they are – then expect friendship to suffer too.

Friendship also requires trust, a presumption on both sides of honesty and virtue. When trust and honesty and the related concept and practice of honour are threatened then friendship is threatened too. Earlier chapters have given several instances of the preference in modern society for explicit written guarantees and procedures over trust especially in politics and business. Even more important, friendship is a variety of love. And about love we also find confusion and inarticulateness today.

SENTIMENTALITY AND FRIENDSHIP

John Henry Newman has already been cited to the effect that love is a practice. To talk about it is not to do it. There is plenty of talk about love today. A thousand and one greetings cards protest love. But not only is that inconclusive evidence of love, it is also, in many cases, pretty simplistic talk. Of all the virtues love is most prone to sentimentalisation. Feelings of "love" can become an exquisite personal indulgence, feelings indulged for their own sake rather than for their objects' sake or for their results, feelings indulged for the pleasure they give to oneself rather than to the person allegedly loved. The test of love for another is what I will do for him or her not what I feel like. There is no reason why friendship, like other loves, should not have external markings for others to see. Indeed, as I have argued, friendship needs more external signs and public acknowledgment, but friendship is not done for effects, for the delight of seeing oneself being a friend.

If there has been a decline in virtue and friendship then one cause is the rise of sentimentality and it is a cause which serves to obscure the decline. For sentimentality is a trade in fakes.[92] It does not openly attack virtue or friendship, it substitutes something which superficially looks like them. Sentimentality is a feeling, or rather the distortion of a feeling, deep in the psyche of western civilisation. And this same corruption of feeling is the key to threats to religion and morals, to music and literature, to the relief of pain and suffering by medicine and charity and to the sensible conservation of the earth. Sentimentalism can capture an entire nation. Writing

---

[92] Digby Anderson and Peter Mullen (eds), *Faking it: the sentimentalisation of modern society*, Social Affairs Unit, London, 1998

about the funeral of the Princess of Wales, Diana, child-like in her self-centredness, Professor Anthony O'Hear finds that funeral the very definition of sentimentality, "the elevation of feelings, image, spontaneity over reason, reality and restraint."[93]

In a recent analysis of sentimentality,[94] the authors found the sentimentalist refusing sound judgement in medicine, chasing miracle cures, defying cancers, indulging himself in revelatory counselling. He is there in the medical commentator undermining the necessity for doctors to make judgements. He is a pedlar of utopias. The sentimental environmentalist is determined that his utopia shall not be prevented by equivocal or even hostile scientific evidence, or by cost. The sentimentalist bestrides gigantic social engineering projects such as affirmative action, impatient that numerical quotas of income be met and contemptuous of the discrepant natures of those he regards as a homogeneous group. In modern music the sentimentalist indulges himself with no sense of humour. In the modern novel he fakes feelings and he even fakes having no feelings. At the dinner table he disguises his childish whims as he rejects good food under modish isms. All through, he is a poseur affecting compassion and emotion to the point of self-deception. He conjures illusions in front of the looking-glass. His aim is not understanding, sociability, truth, social betterment or even genuine feeling, though that is its superficial appearance. It is self-image.

When sentimentalists have their way with an education policy or a welfare policy, with literature or music, with religion and even with pleasures such as eating and drinking, they drain them of substance, cut them off from reality and leave only a corpse pleasantly scented but rotting within. The letters to an agony aunt discussed in a previous chapter, as well as numerous surveys especially among young people, show there is much current approval for friendship.

---

[93] *Ibid* p 184
[94] *Ibid*

The question is whether the thing approved of is the genuine article or a fake. Thus the decline of friendship is tied to the loss of virtue in that both virtue and friendship are corrupted by the same tendency to sentimentality.

THE LOSS OF MANNERS[95]

The loss of manners resembles the loss of virtue in several ways and differs from it in one very important way. The loss could be, as with virtue, a loss not only of behaviour but vocabulary. We may be worse mannered and we may no longer understand the role of manners very well. However one reason manners are dismissed by some today is that, unlike virtue, they are seen as small matters or surface phenomena, mere outward show, form. In fact bad manners, though often individually "trivial", may together make a neighbourhood unliveable in and may coarsen and degrade public space and life. Some manners are the outward manifestation of internal morals. Even when they are not, when they are simply mechanical, it may be that the lack of trivial manners causes more social damage and unhappiness than the lack of heroic morals. This is difficult to accept. Long before the 1960s, the triviality of manners had been derided by those who prided themselves on thinking big; it is traceable at least as far back as Rousseau. There was only one term of abuse stronger than bourgeois and that was petit-bourgeois with its connotations, in English use, of the trite and unimaginative. The decadent 1890s, Freud (or rather his disciples), Bloomsbury, the Marxists, and the flowering of them all in the 1960s, could at least agree on this: their contempt for little men and their mindless daily habits, their manners. Some of them did not have overmuch time for morals either, but at least morals were about big things.

And there is a set of qualities which are part morals, part manners, especially likely to be dismissed as trivial. I am thinking of words such as reticence, reserve, discretion, diffidence and amateurishness.

---

[95] Digby Anderson (ed), *Gentility recalled*, Social Affairs Unit, London, 1996

Some have even been re-cast as quasi-illnesses in a "therapeutic society". They are by their very nature quiet virtues and tacit virtues. They are practised, known but not discussed.

Friendship shares with manners and the quiet virtues this un-discussed, tacit character and this reputation of being a small thing, though not for the same reason. "Small" is perhaps not the right word; better perhaps is "of no public concern". Friendship like manners can be safely ignored by those not immediately involved. It is not like the law, parliament, the family, even the community – something to be concerned about. At least that is the modern view when the modern person finds time to think about manners or friendship at all. Both manners and friendship are victims of this modern belittling tendency. For on any historical test both manners and friendship are big things, both capable of stirring emotions and actions.

CONCLUSION

Friendship today has its own problems. But it seems that some of its difficulties it shares with other institutions such as morality and manners. The trouble all three are in may help in explaining the cause of decline. Surely the elevation of freedom and choice way above virtue by both left and right is dangerous for both virtue and friendship. But it also has another implication. When we start to add up the factors that allow us to estimate the worth of our modern society, along with the gains, especially the materialistic gains of longer, healthier and richer lives, we must set not one but at least three losses: the loss of virtue, of manners and of friendship and of the understanding of all three. Aristotle wondered whether a life without friendship was worth living. We can restate the question: Is a longer, healthier and richer life without friends, virtue or manners worth living?

CHAPTER NINE

AT AND BEYOND THE MARGINS OF FRIENDSHIP: COTERIES, FRIENDLY SOCIETIES AND FREEMASONS

FRIENDSHIP UNNOTICED

Recently a French friend died. It was somewhat unexpected, a cancer diagnosed in the summer, the death in September. He was in his fifties. I had been down with him after the diagnosis partly to see him, to chat, joke, eat and drink and cheer him up but partly and rather more selfishly, because of where he lived. Most summers I visited him there for Bouzigues is such a pleasant place to visit. It is, now, an overgrown village on the French Mediterranean. To be more precise, the village is on a sea-water lake at the back of the Mediterranean port of Sète. Both oysters and mussels are cultivated in the lake and Sète is one of the premier fishing ports of France. The area nearby produces the most if not the best wine in France and Provence to the east produces the fruit and vegetables. So it's sun, sea, swimming, fishing, good food and lots of wine. Also the village is comparatively unspoilt. There are more restaurants now. When I first knew Claude there weren't any. There are more pleasure boats and fewer wooden fishing boats, even fewer of the fishermen who used to gather clams by scraping the lake bottom with long wooden-handled rakes. But the clams are still coming up somehow and can be bought at Mèze a couple of miles away or negotiated for in the local bar.

I first went there forty years ago. And that was the year I first met Claude. I don't think a year has since passed when I haven't been to Bouzigues. We got on well together, to be sure, as I did with the rest of his family. But I had always supposed that the reason for returning so often was the place. The house was on the little harbour and it is a wonderful place to stay. Seeing him and his family, old acquaintances, was a bonus, but the main reason was the place.

Well, I now know it wasn't. I sensed it first when he was ill. The possibility that he had not long to live was what was needed to make me aware that we were more than good time companions. He was and had been for many years a friend. When he died, and I got a flight down for the funeral three days later, I finally understood what a good friend he had been.

And that is the first point of the story. It seems you can have friends, deep friendships without being aware of it at the time. It is not surprising that funerals and predictions of death bring home to one the extent of true affections. What is surprising is that one can have a friend and a friendship, in this case for nearly forty years and be unaware of it. A theme of this book has been that modern society cannot talk about friendship and does not recognize it as an institution. If my experience is at all common, something even worse is happening; we are so unperceptive of friendship that we cannot even see our friends for what they are, until it is too late.

It is worth considering too how that friendship grew, albeit grew unnoticed. Over the forty years, and after the first year, I saw Claude for a mere two weeks a year. I'd arrive. He'd be on the boat or in the garden with a drink. There would be a perfunctory Gallic embrace, one minute of courtesies, "How was the flight?", "How is the family?" then it was back to where we left off last year, "Are we going fishing tomorrow, do we need more wine from Mont Plaisir? Who is going to open the oysters? How are we going to cook the bass?" And still later in the evening just sitting, watching the people walk up and down on the little harbour, each of us finding the same ones funny, pretentious, bizarre, charming or annoying. Almost everyone I have talked with about friendship has remarked on this; the way, once well-founded it can survive on a few days a year; how it can be frozen for months, even years then be thawed back to life in minutes.

Yet the Claude story has an aspect of much more concern to this chapter, which is about institutions on the edge of friendship. For there are things which, while not friendship, help to start and support friendship and there are things which superficially look like friendship which are not friendship and may even be dangers to it.

When I first went down to Bouzigues it took a full day to get down there from England and it was an exhausting day too. France then, in 1961, was a very different place; not yet what is called a "modern" country; still some horses working in the fields, still some clogs. In those days it was somewhat unusual, an adventure, even rather a reckless adventure for a young Englishman to go off and work there for people he had never met, in a land he knew next to nothing of. I went, as a tutor, to teach two boys, Claude and François, as a private tutor in the family for a year. The family, which was a slightly formal bourgeois family, became like a second family to me and Claude became a special friend.

ROTARY CLUBS AND FRIENDSHIP

The point of the reminiscence is how this friendship came about. I got the job because of two things. First I had become obsessed with all things French after going to see people in a very different part of the country in the north. That had come about because my father's Rotary Club had forged links with a French Rotary Club in Boulogne. I was sent over to stay with one of its members' family and their son came to stay with us. When I wanted to go and work in France, an advertisement was placed in the French Rotarian magazine. Claude's father, a Rotarian, read it and replied.

So both the Francophilia and the job came about through Rotary, and, I suppose, so did the friendship. Then, and I imagine now, intellectuals like to sneer at Rotary. I remember doing a bit of sneering myself. It is an organization which brings together one person from each trade or profession in the town to share a usually indifferent lunch once a week – in France they have a rather better dinner. It does a spot of charity, promotes civil life, and encourages international links. It has no intellectual pretensions. It is uninterested in politics. Even its charity is unheroic. In short it is just the kind of thing intellectuals dislike: complacent, provincial and part of the status quo. Since being provincial and uninterested in politics are not yet crimes, those who disapprove of Rotary and would like to do more than just sneer at it, have had to find something else to charge it with and they have found that in its habit of having Rotary for men and Inner Wheel for ladies. In the USA pressure has been brought and Rotary is now open to women. As with gentlemen's clubs, single sex associations do provide a special basis for friendships and that must now be at risk. The sorts of people who sneer at Rotary are not much bothered, of course, by any such risk.

I am not a Rotarian. But I've known plenty, largely through my family, and there is no doubt it has provided a basis for friendship. The evidence in this book is clear; one cannot contrive friendship. Organizations cannot make friendships happen. Friendships cannot be designed and built. But an organization can bring people together. It can have membership rules which select people of backgrounds and characters likely to be compatible. It can put people of different countries in touch.

Societies such as Rotary – and there are many others – provide a meeting place in which friendships can be formed. So, of course, do schools, universities and clubs, already discussed in earlier chapters. That is about it. These institutions rarely nurture friendship or support it much. Most friendships do that themselves. But the societies do provide initial suitable contact.

FREEMASONS AND FRIENDSHIP

If one values friendship then one will value a society or institution which helps it. It is interesting how the intellectuals get away with sneering at Rotary, and for that matter Freemasons or gentlemen's clubs. It is as if helping friendship were not a task worthy of admiration, indeed deserving of contempt. Recently, in England, the United Grand Lodge of England appointed a public relations agency to counter such sneering. In response the masons' critics organized a television programme making fun of masonic initiation rituals and various newspapers indulged in the other anti-masonic sport of implying that masons help each other at the expense of non-masons. The masons replied that "Freemasons promise to support others in time of need, but only if that support does not conflict with their duties to God, the law, their family or with their responsibilities as a citizen".[96] The majority of the £17 million they collect for charity goes to non-masonic charities.

What is interesting in the dispute is that the masons feel obliged to proclaim their extra-masonic benevolence. What is wrong with helping one's friends? The critics of the lodges are similarly oblivious of any merits in friendship. They anchor the debate about free-

---

[96] *The Guardian*, 21.3.2001

masonry on its rituals, its former secrecy and its mutual aid. No doubt these are worth discussion though it is interesting to see masonry's leftish critics finding mutual aid to be a defect. Once it was a high virtue in socialism. But whatever the merits of these, poor friendship and masonry's possible contribution towards it are not mentioned by either side in the debate. Such is the lack of interest in friendship today.

FRIENDLY SOCIETIES

Rotary makes it clear that the encouragement of friendship is one of its aims, especially the encouragement of international friendship; it is Rotary International. Friendly Societies, of course, actually have the word "friendly" in their name and it might be supposed that they, even more than Rotary, are about friendship. This is not so, or at least not directly. David Beito in his authoritative study of American friendly societies, what are there called fraternal societies,[97] *From mutual aid to welfare state*, distinguishes three functions of such societies: secret association, ritualism and mutual benefit. Ritualism and secrecy would also fit freemasonry – though neither fits Rotary – and so indeed would mutual assurance. And freemasonry and mutual welfare societies have historical origins in common. Beito also quotes the mottos of various societies and they include such words as: unity, temperance, charity, love, purity, wisdom, protection, security, fraternity. Some of these are the same as the virtues which are associated with friendship. The societies aimed to protect their members from a cruel world. One society, for instance, referred to its initiates as "members of the same family" pledged to "stand by one another at all hazards...declaring ourselves brothers and sisters". In later practice this meant largely the sick and the consequences of sickness.

David Green, in an interview, talking of the British friendly societies, points out that they were not directly about friendship, or even love

---

[97] David Beito, *From mutual aid to welfare state*, University of North Carolina Press, 2000

or charity. They went out of their way to distinguish their central objective from charity. Formed in days when it was a real possibility that a family might lose its breadwinner to disease or death, they were about insurance. The insurance was for doctors' bills, for income when a sick husband could not work, and for costs associated with death, funerals and widowhood. In the societies, families pooled their risks and costs. This was not charity or even love but self-protection through mutual insurance.

However, both the origins of the societies and the ways they operated were associated with friendship. The problems the societies solved were exacerbated by migration into the new industrial cities and working sites such as mines and by international immigration in the case of the USA. The very movements which could disconnect migrants and immigrants from material support could also leave them lonely and friendless. Green estimates that many members of the societies came to their meetings seeking friendship and sociability as much as insurance. And the societies did work through meetings at weekly or fortnightly intervals. In their heyday, members were obliged to show up personally to pay their subscriptions. And they did more than just pay dues. The meetings might last an hour or two and members went through initiations into different stages or levels of the society over the years. The rituals associated with these initiations display the societies' values especially those of being a good father, husband and work-colleague. Moreover, offices were rotated so as to involve the largest possible number of members. The members could hardly fail to get to know each other.

Interestingly, in the largest British society, the meeting would be run by a foursome of a chairman, last year's chairman and two others. One of these others was someone well-versed in procedure and he gave the comparatively ignorant new chairman support in expertise. The other, known as the chairman's "left-hand" was nominated by the chairman from among his friends and his task was to give moral support to a shy and inarticulate chairman.

If friendship played a part in procedure, it also played a part after the meeting when the members might stay on to drink – often meetings were held in pubs – sing or recite. Further evidence of the role of friendship can be found in the steps the societies took to counter the vices traditionally associated with friendship gone wrong such as cliques and cabals and improper favouritism. The societies' rules about procedure and book-keeping, and indeed the rotation of offices are evidence that they knew that various personal relationships could arise in societies and took steps to forestall them.

In the first pages of this book we saw that many people die today without friends and also that organizations exist to provide friend-substitutes at sickbeds in modern hospitals. The friendly societies made sure the sick were visited, at least in part to make certain they were indeed sick and thus entitled to draw the society's sick pay. We should not make too much of this. The society's representative was not chosen because he was a friend or to be one. The sick man would know him but not necessarily like him. Similarly society members attended deceased members' funerals or were fined a considerable amount if they did not. Both funeral attendance and sickbed visiting were institutionalised visiting, not, in themselves, friendship.

Nevertheless, the regular meetings of people who shared a way of life and its hazards, their participation in the procedures and rituals, their subscription to common values and their visiting at times of life's sad and trying moments all provided a circumstance in which friendship could be discovered and grow. As with Rotary, they were not enough to make and maintain friendship. That still had to come from the characters of the sets of friends. But they were a basis for mutual attraction to be recognized and sustained.

When we look at the ways organizations such as Rotary or friendly societies or some schools, clubs and churches help friendship, we find two sorts. The first are, from a moral point of view, neutral. They provide introductions of strangers, places to meet, regularity of contact, participation, means of getting to know each other. But they also have various declared virtues which affect who is allowed to join or attend, their conduct during involvement and possibly outside, the way the school or meeting or whatever is done. It is this second sort of function which makes it likely that true friendship and not some other association will result. Of course, any association can grow when people are introduced and kept in touch. No doubt criminal gangs can be formed in schools and church choirs. But at least Rotary, some schools, friendly societies and the others have virtues several of which are closely linked to friendship.

BAD FRIENDS

Good mothers are solicitous for the welfare of their children. And especially middle-class mothers are worried about the other children that their children might mix with. Perhaps less so nowadays, but certainly when I was a child in the forties and fifties, it was thought that bad habits could, rather like the measles, be caught through close contact. "Since you have been playing with Tommy, you've started to speak badly/be rude/ become difficult/ are not the nice child you used to be" were some of the charges. One reason, perhaps the most important reason, why so many such parents struggled to send their children to private schools was the expectation that there they would mix with better children and acquire good habits. Close contact with others can bring out the best in a child, or adult, and the worst. In a school where contact is for entire days for most of the year, and even more in boarding schools where it is for fourteen weeks at a time more or less total, the potential for damage or good to affect character is enormous.

In all this the parents showed a good understanding of "peer group pressure" *avant la lettre.*

The close contact at school can make both for good and bad friendships. The notion of bad friendships is, given the way friendship has been used so far, a contradiction in terms. If friendship is something built on mutual virtue in which each brings out the morally best in the other, then bad friendships cannot exist. What I mean by that term then is not a friendship but something which has some of the associative and affective attributes of friendship; the two people see each other a lot, exchange confidences, help each other. But since neither has a commitment to goodness not only will they not be good but they may well bring out the worst in each other.

The concern of mothers that their children mix with the right sort of other children became, especially in the Sixties, an object of scorn, humour and even indignation among progressive intellectuals. This was a time in England when schools were being comprehensivised, that is, were meant to take their pupils simply from a catchment area instead of selecting them according to intellect or character or social background. Some intellectuals objected to the criteria previously used for selection, some to selection itself. Some pointed out that parents and schools had been using background, social class, accent, clothing, notions of "respectability" to select pupils and schools.

It is true that character is not something which is easy to detect and some schools and parents may have used surrogates which were unreliable indicators of it. But, often appearances, clothes, manners, speech are the only ways to detect character. The judgments of parents about whom it was desirable that their children should mix with may have been wrong on occasions. But to the parents they were important, even necessary. In contrast most progressive intellectuals washed their hands of the whole business of mixing, character formation and friendship. Many of them in education, psychology and criminology still do. Yet another instance in which they show no interest in friendship.

FRIENDSHIP IN TERRORIST AND DELINQUENT GANGS

But that still leaves us with the matter of "bad friends" or "bad friendships". What sense can be made of them? The problem arises in part because we use the language of friendship today both to describe friends in the high Aristotelian sense and to mean companions. Indeed all sorts of non-friends, even enemies can, on occasions be "friendly". In this case, the enemy may be behaving as if he were a friend (when he is not) or "friendly" may simply mean "pleasant company". In other cases we might mean something much stronger. Consider the case of a teenage boy who is friends with three other teenage boys. Together they are louts. They are rude, fight with other boys, get drunk, take drugs and occasionally steal. They are bad boys. But when they get into trouble, they do not betray each other. They are, amongst themselves, trustworthy, loyal and brave. Are they then friends, united in and by virtue? In the high sense, certainly not.

This is similar to the case raised by E M Forster, mentioned in an earlier chapter. Forster said that if he had to choose between betraying his country and betraying his friend, he hoped he would have the courage to betray his country. Aristotle, as Andrew Sullivan rightly remarks,[98] would have found this remark

> *"nonsensical. Cicero would have found it contemptible.*
> *Both would have been right. A true friend will never*
> *put his friend in a moral dilemma; he will not ask him*
> *to do what is wrong or ask him to place their friendship*
> *before the common good, or demand that he lie for*
> *him, or make excuses for him."*

---

[98] Andrew Sullivan, *Love undetectable, op cit*, pp 221-3

185

Sullivan quotes Cicero:

> *"Alliance of wicked men not only shouldn't be protected*
> *by a plea of friendship, but rather they should be visited*
> *with summary punishment of the severest kind, so that*
> *no one may think it permissible to follow even a friend*
> *when waging war against his own country."*

and Aelred:

> *"Love is shameful and unworthy of the name of*
> *friendship wherein anything foul is demanded of a*
> *friend...We should detest the opinion of those who*
> *think that one should act on behalf of a friend in any*
> *way detrimental to faith and uprightness. For it is no*
> *excuse for sin, that you sin for the sake of a friend."*

Others have gone further. When what appear to be virtuous dispositions such as loyalty and courage are enlisted in the service of vice, the vice may be worse, at least in its effects. Discussing the terrorism of the IRA, Gerald Frost writes,

> *"It is the combination of misdirected virtue and vice,*
> *of self-denial and murderous ruthlessness which makes*
> *the IRA such a formidable threat. If its leaders were*
> *engaged in wickedness for its own sake, it is unlikely*
> *that they would have been sufficiently patient and*
> *single-minded to acquire the organizational, fund-*
> *raising and public relations skills required by a modern*
> *terrorist campaign...The personal qualities which*
> *the Irish terrorists have brought to their campaign*
> *have also enabled them to forge a strong sense of*
> *community..."*

Frost goes on to pin-point the besetting and key vice in those who would tie their loyalty and courage to evil ends. It is, of course, the vice of pride and arrogance.[99]

---

[99] Gerald Frost (ed), *Loyalty misplaced*, Social Affairs Unit, London, 1997, p xiii

True friendship, then is not characterized simply by neutral matters such as frequent association or even by the display of certain special virtues such as loyalty and trust, important as they may be. It is a union of two or more virtuous people. It may seem as if this is just an argument about a word. Why shouldn't we use "friend" to describe both a virtuous friend and the loutish member of a teenage delinquent gang? Does it matter if the friendship is used to describe a life-long moral attachment and a nodding acquaintance-ship made over dinner or at a party last Saturday? Probably not, provided the users of the word remember the crucial differences. But then, is not the elasticated usage of friendship itself a sign of a society that does not understand what (high) friendship means in conversation and in practice?

GROUPS OF FRIENDS – THE APOSTLES

One does not have to go to the lengths of terrorist gangs, political or criminal, to see "bad friendships" or simply false friendships. Take the friendships of intellectuals, those of Bloomsbury or among the de Beauvoir-Sartre set after the Second World War in France. Do these merit the term friendship? There can be little doubt that Oxbridge academics such as Oscar Browning, Goldsworthy Lowes Dickinson (teacher of E M Forster of the friend versus country remark) and Maurice Bowra had individual friendships and rated friendship very highly.[100] And, in an earlier chapter, we have seen that small groups of academics such as the Inklings – Tolkien, C S Lewis, Charles Williams *et al* were certainly sets of friends in the sense that each of four or five of them were friends of most if not all the others. What is much more questionable is whether societies and coteries such as the Apostles or Bloomsbury can be described as groups of friends.

Members of the Bloomsbury set certainly spent time and passions, intellectual and otherwise, together. In an interview in 2001, the

---

[100] Noel Annan, *The dons, op cit*

longest surviving Bloomsbury member, Frances Partridge, then aged 101, talked of the others. She "fell for" E M Forster. Maynard Keynes "threw wonderful parties...Duncan Grant was enormously charming." They were indeed a "set". Some such as Ottoline Morrell helped others financially. Members of the set took up with other members only to drop them a year or two later. The story of Bloomsbury is much more one of lust, jealousy, rivalry, betrayal, attempts at dominance, deceit, and self-indulgence than it is of friendship. Indeed in that long interview it is difficult to find one reminiscence that could justify her claim that Bloomsbury was "about friendship and truth".[101]

The Apostles, a semi-secret society founded at Cambridge, has been known for many things. It has been a recruiting ground for the intellectual aristocracy, a nurturer of intellectual talent, a mutual advancement society, a source of homosexual protection and among a few of its members, a source of communist subversion. Alan Ryan says that the Apostles were devoted to two things, friendship and intellectual honesty and he speaks of their "cult of friendship".[102] Certainly they thought of themselves in this way and even as reviving classical friendship. Though the founders included evangelicals, by Forster's time they were much more attached to what they saw as classical ideals of friendship. But there is certainly little Aristotelian in their refusal to be bound by the obligations to their country or city or society and the virtues. Indeed some of them put their various loyalties to each other above that to the country.

Nor did the Apostles come together in some organic way, they did not grow together as friends do. They were selected and elected. New recruits – "eggs" – were identified and "hatched". The criteria for election were not the virtues of friendship but intellectual brilliance. Nor, subsequent to recruitment, did the Apostles behave like a group of friends. Though of course individual Apostles did

---

101 *The Times* (London), 3.17.2001
102 *London Review of Books*, 28.10.1999, pp 18-19

make friends with other individual Apostles, the society is much better seen as a society for conversation, mutual advancement and admiration and influence than a group of friends.

Sartre and Camus, for a while, regarded themselves as friends. Sartre more than once uses the term of Camus, though notably in the past tense. They, for a time, shared what they thought was a moral vision. But Sartre's treatment of Camus after the publication of *L'Homme Revolté* was not the act of a friend. It is instructive that of their several disagreements, it was Camus' honesty in wishing to confront Soviet crimes and Sartre's immoral acrobatics in refusing to face and tell the truth, that was the occasion of the end of the friendship. It is somehow fitting that Sartre's betrayal of an intellectual's calling to pursue truth, and his betrayal of those in need of political championship should occasion his break with Camus and his and Francis Jeanson's polemical mugging of Camus in *Les Temps Modernes*. The story has been told well for instance both by Tony Judt in his study of modern French intellectual life[103] and by Camus' biographer, Olivier Todd.[104] It may well be that this book has been somewhat hard on modern friendships, that is, on ordinary peoples' friendships. But it is difficult to be too harsh about the claims of Bloomsbury, the Apostles and the Sartre coterie to be considered friendships.

FRATERNITE: FORCED FRIENDSHIP

If some of the Apostles are beyond friendship then so is the idea of fraternity. One of the words which runs through the American literature on mutual aid societies is "fraternity". It means treating someone like a brother. Aristotle, it will be remembered thought of friends as people with the rights and obligations of kin, people like brothers. It may be that the word is justified in its use by the mutuals. But its relationship with friendship is more problematic. Fraternity, of course, long ago entered the political dictionary as

---

103 Tony Judt, *Past imperfect: French intellectuals 1944-56*, University of California Press, 1992
104 Olivier Todd, *Albert Camus: A life*, Vintage, London, 1998

fraternité and there it is certainly not justified. For the essence of the political ideal of fraternity is that all men are our brothers – or, in a variation, that all men of the same social class are our brothers. Mankind is a brotherhood. In this use of fraternity-friendship there is no element of choice. All men are to be our friends and brothers. It is a right and obligation.

But friendship which is coerced is not friendship. Peter Mullen once made a protest against the use of the word "community" as in "the gay community" or "the black community".[105] Homosexual people may have several things in common as may black people. It is possible, though unlikely, that they may all share the same political interest and can be represented by some lobby or interest group. They may, though it is also unlikely, all share one style of life. But a community is more than a political interest group or a lifestyle shared, it means people who regularly interact with each other and often know each other face-to-face quite well. It is a warm-hearted word. Friendship is an even warmer word. Friendship is freely chosen, not dictated by commissars or rights theorists. It involves the growing together of two people; their union in a common moral life, as Aristotle saw it; the mutual attraction of two personalities following Montaigne. At the very least, friends spend time together. A political grouping as indicated by the politicized use of "fraternity" has none of these things. Friendship cannot be an obligation. At least a particular friendship cannot be an obligation, nor can men be obliged to be friends with all.

The Russian Revolution, its legacy and its vocabulary and rhetoric are now largely discredited. But for progressive people, the French Revolution is still seen as a liberating event. No progressive person is ashamed of its slogan, "Liberté, Egalité, Fraternité". From its birth and precipitate prophetic baptism in blood it has furnished the two key terms of progressive political debate, liberty and equality.

---

[105] Peter Mullen, "Community" in D Anderson (ed), *The dictionary of dangerous words*, Social Affairs Unit, London, 2000

But what of the third member of the trio? Fraternité, like the other two, was, and presumably is for the heirs of the French Revolution, a political project. Its derivatives are seen in the political imposition of the titles "Citoyen", "Brother" and "Comrade" and there are echoes of it in the rhetoric of the various "rights" lobbies. It is there, as I say, in the alleged requirement of oppressed minorities such as blacks to find that all other blacks are their brothers, comrades and friends. More speculatively, modern attempts to impose counselling, state-sanctioned friendships, have the smell of fraternité. The revolutionary fraternité tends to universalism. It anticipated later forms of internationalism. It was certainly not about friendship or small craft and professional camaraderie. Though fraternité could be massaged to support French revolutionary patriotism, it was essentially a brotherhood of peoples across national boundaries, a sort of internationalism which subverted national loyalties.

Now there is a necessary political element to liberty; freedom needs the safeguard of laws, the policing and punishment of its abuse in the denial of others' freedom. The state's part in securing equality is more controversial; though most would agree with some state action in ensuring equality before the law and perhaps of representation. But it is when we consider the politicisation of fraternité that we see something deeply implausible.

One of the few nineteenth century thinkers to think critically about fraternité was James Fitzjames Stephen.[106] He spotted its coercive character immediately. He confessed to feelings of disgust when confronted with the slogan "fraternité", and expected other sensible people to be similarly affected. "I know hardly anything in literature so nauseous as Rousseau's expressions of love for mankind," he wrote: "Keep your love to yourself, and do not daub me or mine with it." The nineteenth century Cardinal Newman can aptly be re-quoted here: "How absurd it is when writers talk magnificently

---

[106] James Fitzjames Stephen, *Liberty, equality, fraternity*, University of Chicago Press, Chicago, 1991, first page of "Fraternity"

about loving the whole human race…That is not to love men, it is but to talk of love. The love of real men depends on practice [and that must start not with "abstractions" or "expansive benevolence"] but by "cultivating an intimate friendship with those immediately about us".

Is not "loving the whole human race" or, rather, talking about loving the whole human race what modern rights talk and the assorted United Nations acronyms are about? Newman thought it absurd precisely because it was a slogan. It still is a universalistic slogan not based in practice and particular affection. If human dignity is based on this, then it is indeed precariously based. Stephen agreed but he added something else. Before he was prepared to love all men, someone must show him why, he said. There was only one reason that anyone would be likely to attempt such love for the human race and that was because it was divinely commanded. And the very people who so insisted on universalistic fraternité denied God's existence and, he might have added, were busy guillotining His priests.

A little thought shows the danger of politicising relationships such as brotherhood, friendship and family, and indeed the use of terms such as "care" drawn from one sphere for the other. There is something doubly dodgy about state-controlled "community care". But further reflection shows that even non-political universalistic fraternity is suspect. One hears much about Christianity's command to love all men. But it is not that simple. As Newman pointed out, "any" man is probably a better formulation than "all men". Even that is wrong because we should not interpret that to mean "any man I choose". Sons are called on to love their mothers. Other peoples' mothers won't do. In fact Christianity is even less fraternal than this. For in its scheme of things, fraternité is not a direct virtue. Christianity does not command its members directly to love one another. It has no horizontal – man to man – conception of human love and dignity and no autonomous teaching of human brotherhood. Its members are not to love one another because they are fellow humans; but because they are all in the image and after the likeness of God, in flesh sanctified by God's taking of flesh and because they are fellow sons of God. It is not fraternité but paternité which is the cornerstone. The central Christian virtues are vertical not horizontal. We are to love and respect others because we love and obey God and He loves them. Look at the Ten Commandments and you will see that they start with commands about duty to God. From this follows and depends duty to men.

This is reinforced by later Christian teaching about "divine adoption". St Paul explains that all men are adopted sons of God. He becomes father to all and thus all are heirs to his riches. But whether the doctrine be about natural or adopted family, its slogan could well be, "No fraternité without paternité". No human dignity, mutual esteem and respect, no human rights, without God. Dump the Father and you dump the brother. Or else you must find some other reason to respect the brother. In Stephen's words, "If [the believer in fraternity] wants me to love all mankind, he must show me why."

So the first basis of human dignity in the Christian tradition is the common paternity of a Christian God. I would add that the Christian idea of fraternity is also a good deal more practical than the sentimental notions of human rights. It allows me, or you, to disapprove of what your brother does, even dislike what he has become, provided you remember who he is. It in no way confuses loving with liking.

HOMOSEXUALITY

The fourth matter at or beyond the margins of friendship is homosexuality.

There's no reason to suppose that men who find other men sexually attractive are any more or less likely to have male friends than men who find women sexually attractive. What can interfere with friendship however is an excessive, uncontained pursuit of sex, either hetero- or homosexual. Most people think of themselves as complex identities, someone's son or daughter, a doctor or a factory worker, coming from the town or country, the north or the south, interested in darts or deep-sea diving. One factor in this complex identity is sexual attraction.

Another way to put it is that most people, while acknowledging that they are sometimes and on some occasions attracted to the opposite or the same sex do not make that the definition of their identity. They do not think of themselves as "a heterosexual" or "a homosexual". A minority does think of itself in this way and they are encouraged to do so, in the case of persons with homosexual inclinations, by homosexual political activism. This aims to turn an inclination into a way of life.

Both hetero- and homosexually inclined persons have the task of keeping their inclinations from damaging their friendships. If sexual preoccupation is not contained either because of a macho, promiscuous heterosexual way of life or a politically driven homosexual identity, then friendship is in trouble. The failure to contain inclinations can have exactly the same results as its archenemy, a certain sort of cold manliness. The latter regards male friendships as dangerous. It is especially worried about signs of affection and obsessed with relationships becoming "effeminate". At its crudest, it thinks close male friendships always harbour the danger of homosexuality. The homosexual activists agree though they relish the prospect rather than disapprove of it.

What friendship needs from society is a recognition that it is a relationship which is complete in its own right. It is not, if it goes too far, going to topple into homosexuality. A strong, deep friendship is not somehow "nearer" homosexuality than a weak, passing companionship. It neither needs sexual attraction, still less sexual fulfillment, to be complete nor does it "lead" to either of them. A sexually obsessed society, be the obsession liberational or repressive, is the enemy of friendship.

In the first chapter I referred to a newspaper obituary editor who explained the absence of references to friendship in obituaries. One of his two explanations was that readers might construe emphasis on the dead person's friendships to be a coded allusion to his homosexuality. The reason for using a code could be that the society is so prudish that it cannot name the relationship for what it was. Or it might be, and this is far worse and more likely, that it cannot admit of a deep relationship that is neither familial nor sexual. One way or another poor friendship suffers.

CHAPTER TEN

CONCLUSION: A FUTURE FOR FRIENDSHIP?

Whether high friendship survives depends on what sort of society countries such as Britain and America become. For friendship is not just the fruit of two individuals' attraction to each other. It needs certain things from the society itself. The first of these things is a certain disposition in ethics, politics and religion. At the risk of oversimplification and over theorization it is possible to sketch out three social stages or ideas: the classical, the Christian and the modern-secular – and their links with friendship. In the classical friendship is a virtue, an end not a means. As such it reinforces and is reinforced by other virtues. Classical friendship unambiguously prefers the particular to the universal – whether of love or right. In the classical nature is triumphant.

In the Christian tradition, earthly friendship is a virtue to the degree that it is compatible with love of the divine and the eternal, and the command to universal love: Christians have been divided over this compatibility. Though it is ultimately subordinated to man's eternal destiny, it is only ultimately so. We may have no abiding city on this earth but most Christians, contemplative religious apart, are meant to be actively involved in making this world a better place. Christianity recognizes our nature but is not content with it.

In the secular, friendship is not a virtue. It is a means not an end. It is in tension with high ideals of secular rights and duty often linked to utopian schemes which subordinate nature to right, and which emphasize egalitarian right. The effect of the move from the classical through the Christian to the modern-secular is to diminish all the virtues and to delegitimize friendship. A further effect is that form of social disorder which comes from the failure to perceive that particular good will (i.e. friendship) is, in fact vitally necessary for the success of universal ideals.

In short there are ideas and ideologies in modern society which are hostile or indifferent to friendship. These ideas have seeped into various social institutions and together with other developments have made some of those institutions – modern marriage-divorce and re-marriage is such institution – hostile to or in rivalry with friendship. Friendship is being ousted from the important part it played in business life, university life, military life and professional life. In an age where the virtues have been sentimentalized, friendship too has been sentimentalized. We no longer understand what it is and we give little public place and acknowledgment to it.

I believe something like this explanation is broadly right. But in one respect it hits the wrong note. If particular affection, the love of wife or friend, is a necessary part of what Newman calls the practice of love and if individual friendships, far from being opposed to good political or religious ideals, are a necessary part of them, then it follows that a society which admits and recognizes friendship will have to do more than admit and encourage the idea of friendship. It is the practice that matters. It is no accident that the friendship literature has few theories about friendship but is stuffed with stories of actual friends. I have mentioned a few in this book. Here is one more which concerns me and a friend.

ON THE SHOOT

It is evening time in England in late summer time. As the light fades, a keen eye can just make out the shapes of two men standing with their backs to a wood. They are facing a field of stubble which only recently was harvested of its wheat. They are standing about thirty yards apart, more or less motionless and being as quiet as they can.

Behind the trees, at their backs are some ponds. The two men are waiting for the duck to fly in at the end of the day. When the duck come the men will shoot, if they are lucky, a couple each, before the rest of the duck fly off, circle round and come in to the ponds another and safer way. From the time the men spot the duck to the time the surviving ducks fly away there may be only seconds to try and hit them. Hence the expectation.

The view they have of the darkening countryside is a beautiful one. But the pleasure of it is enhanced by the expectation of sport and all that pleasure is the better for being taken together: two people, two friends, appreciating the beauty in the same way, looking expectantly into the skies in the same way, knowing what each other is thinking and feeling and afterwards, walking back across the fields chatting and joking about the one that was missed, and, less often, the high one that was skillfully hit.

Thirty years later, the two are still at it, though now mostly pheasant shoots. Still that leaves them standing with backs to woods looking for the clatter and rising flight of birds disturbed by beaters and spaniels. Not much gets said on these occasions. There's no need to say much. Once again it's the common experience of countryside and purpose leavened by over thirty years of friendship. Other people's enthusiasms may be boring. But I am sure what can be said of duck shooting can be said of mountaineering, pot holing or sailing.

IN THE PUB

If the friendship grew shooting, it owed nothing to shooting for its start. The credit for that can go to the pub. It was not a very special pub; just a local pub whose customers met on their way home from work. And the third help to the friendship was dinner, lots of dinners. I am not talking here about formal dinner parties but just two or three couples getting together in one of their houses to eat and drink. It is not only that pubs and dinners help friendships grow, they also act as filters, tests if you like. After a few drinks together, a dinner together, one finds out whether these people are indeed the sort one can get on with, as do they with you. And if they are not, there is nothing lost.

It is clear that organizations, such as Rotary, expressly set up to encourage friendship, can successfully do so in that they can provide circumstances which make the formation and to a lesser extent, the maintenance of friendships more likely. They can't make friendships – only friends can do that – but they can provide a place and occasion for people to meet and select people for those occasions who might share sympathetic outlooks.

Other institutions, ones not expressly set up to encourage friendship, can do the same thing. Going through a trial, discipline, grief, pain or discomfort together, especially when isolated can be fertile ground for friendship. This is the psychology exploited by corporations in the current vogue for bonding excursions. A business group is taken off climbing or whatever for a weekend in the hope that common exposure to hardship and danger will bring them closer together and even lead to acts of mutual support. This, of course, is designed to produce, not friendship, but a team. It might even be said to have gone wrong if particular friendships emerged from it, especially if a new twosome got closer and drew further from their companions.

But the circumstances which most promote friendship are expectation, excitement, danger or hardship shared in comparative isolation. Some sports, those which have two or three people split off together are more likely to produce this than eleven-a-side games. Nor does it have to be a sport. It can be two people with a common threat at work, two people both looking after a vulnerable third person, two neighbours with a common problem in a third neighbour.

Pubs, bars, cafes and – already discussed, clubs – may not have much hardship or danger, but they too have special characteristics conducive to friendship. They too provide a place, an occasion. And a lubrication. Less obviously they also select a clientele. In a strict legal sense they are places open to all. But it rarely works out like this. English pubs used to have physically separate bars for different customers, a saloon bar with a carpet, a public bar, once with sawdust, a small private bar, sometimes a games room, a jug bar for people to come in and collect beer to take away. In practice this was often used by women on their own who stayed and had a drink while their jug was filled. The bars attracted people at least partly on the basis of social class, as did different pubs. The walls between the bars have been largely torn down today but often pubs will retain different areas which attract different people. Groups of acquaintances and friends "colonize" areas of pubs which other customers grow to recognize as "theirs".

I go to a pub which – not unusually – also has different sorts of people at different times. Older middle-class men come in early in the evening; lower-class and younger people rather later. This is partly related to the fact that the middle class in England – and in many countries – dine later than the lower classes and tend to drink before rather than after their evening meal. Young people go out later than older people and even have a culture in which staying out late is a mark of pride. The different types of people with their own different times are recognized by the pub landlord who puts pop music and television on for the later customers but not the former.

I have even seen barmen alter their public personalities to suit different cohorts of drinkers. Thus on a buffet car bar on a train which stopped first at a station frequented by businessmen commuters and after at one used by homosexual weekenders, I have seen a bar man talk share prices and weather to his businessmen customers for the first 30 miles, then engage in camp talk with the homosexuals when the first group had left. One such barman also changed his voice and name. He was "George" for the first few miles and "Georgie, dear", for the rest.

If you take a small town, add up the different spaces in each pub, multiply them by the cohorts and shifts which come in at different times and multiply that by the thirty or so pubs any small market town will have, you get some idea of the number of different people one can select to be with or avoid. And what is true of pubs is, to a somewhat lesser extent, true of parks, beaches, shopping malls, fitness centres and other places where customers can take over space but also move about.

Groups of already established friends can make temporary homes in such spaces. But one can also make friends in pubs, or rather, pubs offer contacts with new people with, initially, few obligations. Getting into conversation with someone in a pub has nothing like the commitment and hazard of inviting them into one's home. If one finds one has made a mistake, one simply moves away or leaves. So, after tentative soundings, friendships can be built up. The process can also be speeded up when, in a group of drinkers, a friend introduces his other friend.

All this may be absurdly obvious. But it should be noted that it works because pub customers tacitly agree that it should work like this and obey the rules, most of the time. There are also pubs where this happens more than others and it is certainly possible that it could cease happening. Some argue it is happening less today already. One should not take pubs' and bars' services to friendship for granted. It also works because it caters for differences between people – on the basis of age, class, style, interests – which already exist in the wider society. Friendship is helped by the pre-selection of people who are likely to find things in common. Sociologists call this the social stratification system. They don't call it the class system because people can be stratified by age or sex as well as occupation and income. But in common parlance it is a class system in the sense that people of similar ages, incomes, interests tend to spend time together and enjoy doing so. It is both complex and negotiable. But it is also, I think, essential. Friendship is greatly helped by a society which has a system of social differentiation, a sophisticated class system.

There is one other service bars offer to friendship that needs mention and that is alcohol. There is a long tradition in friendship literature of linking it with drinking and eating. There can be no doubt that the exchange of confidences so characteristic of friendship is eased by alcohol. There is a generosity of spirit essential to friendship which comes from the conviviality of a good dinner table. One should not play down the physical effects of alcohol in all this. But there is more: in their different ways, the bar and the dinner party offer well-known calibrated routes for strangers to become acquaintances, occasional companions and sometimes, eventually friends. The sort of pub I have described and the dinner party are as much part of a civilized society as the high arts.

The point is that a change in our ideas about friendship will not save friendship though it can help. Friendship depends on what people do in pubs and clubs, on their birthdays, in their obituaries, at someone's sick bed and funeral, in a will, in business, at school, out fishing, at dinner.

The danger is that these practices, the bits and pieces of everyday life are losing the friendship factor. That is making them far less enjoyable activities. It is also killing friendship where it really counts. What would happen to the occasions and pastimes of friendship without it? There are already pubs and bars which are simply drinking places for solitary people and miserable places they are. There is no reason why strangers should not have a dinner together but they will never have the evening six friends will have even if the menu is identical. Of course you can shoot duck on your own but I think you, or at least I might do it less often. It is the obligation you made to the friend to go out together on Friday that gets you out of the arm chair and across the fields. So Augustine had it right. Doing something on your own which you enjoyed previously with your friend is a thin and even bitter experience:

> *"All that we had done together was now a grim ordeal*
> *without him. My eyes searched everywhere for him,*
> *but he was not there to be seen. I hated all the places*
> *we had known together, because he was not in them."* [107]

WHAT FRIENDSHIP NEEDS FROM A SOCIETY

If one cannot make an individual friend at will, one certainly cannot build a society full of friendship. It helps if there are institutions of work and leisure which provide for like-minded people to meet. It may even require that society sets up organizations expressly for that purpose. It needs a society which promotes the virtues especially those on which friendship depends, those of candour,

---

[107] S. Augustine, *Confessions, op cit* IV. 4

selflessness, fidelity and trust. But more generally that society must have an idea of the good and be committed to it. It will be further committed to a system of manners which spells out the implications of its morals for specific situations. Such a society will also recognize the value of friendship and welcome it in institutions of high status, in business, politics. It will acknowledge the importance of friendship just as it does that of marriage. It will be able to talk explicitly and clearly about friendship and thus be able to recognize the difference between it and unvirtuous pretenders such as cabals, sentimental associations and flatterers. But none of this will help unless the moral life of this society is suffused throughout its daily trivial activities.

Does it matter if society has fewer friendships, true friendships? After all it's a society where people are richer than ever before, lead longer and healthier lives and, in the west, have more democracy than ever before. The problem is that Aristotle might turn out to be right when he said that no sensible person would reckon any of these things were as good as a good friend.[108]

---

[108] Aristotle, *The ethics of Aristotle, op cit*, p 258

PUBLICATIONS FROM THE SOCIAL AFFAIRS UNIT

THE DICTIONARY OF DANGEROUS WORDS
Compiled by Digby Anderson
*"This book will shortly replace a university education.
And it's cheaper."*
John Cleese

FAKING IT: THE SENTIMENTALISATION OF MODERN SOCIETY
Edited by Digby Anderson & Peter Mullen
"The more people who read this book the better."
Chris Woodhead in *Sunday Telegraph*

**GENTILITY RECALLED:
'MERE' MANNERS AND THE MAKING OF SOCIAL ORDER**
Edited by Digby Anderson
*"I wanted to know why the world had changed so much and I got
the answer from Gentility Recalled."*
Bernard Levin in *The Times*

**COME BACK MISS NIGHTINGALE:
TRENDS IN THE PROFESSIONS TODAY**
Edited by Digby Anderson
*"Rightly laments the professions' descent from yesterday's bastion of
morality to today's knowledge factor."*
Leader in *The Daily Telegraph*

**NOT FIT TO FIGHT: THE CULTURAL SUBVERSION OF THE
ARMED FORCES IN BRITAIN AND AMERICA**
Edited by Gerald Frost
"Asks uncomfortable questions and states important facts."
Peter Hitchens in *The Express*

*"The Social Affairs Unit is famous for driving its coach and horses
through the liberal consensus, scattering intellectual picket lines as it
goes. It is equally famous for raising questions which strike most people
most of the time as too dangerous or too difficult to think about."*
The Times